freshwater fish

freshwater fish

MALCOLM GREENHALGH

ILLUSTRATED BY STUART CARTER

MITCHELL BEAZLEY

Contents

First published in 1999 by
Mitchell Beazley, an imprint of
Octopus Publishing Group Ltd
2–4 Heron Quays,
London E14 4JP

Text copyright
© 1999 Octopus Publishing Group Ltd

Design copyright
© 1999 Octopus Publishing Group Ltd

A CIP catalogue copy of this book
is available from the British Library.

Executive Editors	Rachael Stock
	Samantha Ward-Dutton
Executive Art Editor	Emma Boys
Project Editor	Anna Nicholas
Designer	Russell Miller
Production	Rachel Staveley
Picture Researcher	Claire Gouldstone
Fish illustrations	Stuart Carter
Habitat illustrations	Rudi Vizi
Locator maps	Hardlines

ISBN 1 84000 144 5

Set in Gill Sans
Printed and bound in China
by Toppan Printing Company Ltd

Introduction

This book describes the freshwater fish of Europe and provides information on their natural history, distribution, habitat and status.

The black fish that appear in the bottom corner of each page give an average length for the specimens that anglers and naturalists are most likely to come across. The number of pharyngeal teeth (see pages 22–23) appears alongside in cyprinids where known.

c.20cm — Pharyngeal teeth: 4 : 4

The maps featured in this book show the distribution and habitat of each fish species, indicating areas where it occurs naturally (light blue) and where it has been introduced (purple).

Introduced species distribution

Indigenous species distribution

In writing this book, I used two sources of information. The first was a mass of textbooks and scientific papers that I slowly sifted through. The second was personal, first-hand experience. From the literature search it was clear that some fish had not been well described, or that their natural history was not too well known. So, having ceased gainful employment on my 40th birthday, I spent much time travelling in search of these lesser known species and checking information on better known species. In the last 13 years I have caught or seen caught, and closely examined alive or freshly killed, 132 out of the 174 species of European freshwater fish. I also researched the commoner cyprinid hybrids and the information given on pages 140–41 is from this work.

One problem has been the definition of what is a species and what is a subspecies. Currently European fish taxonomy, especially in the Balkan and Iberian regions, seems to be dominated by 'splitters' trying to split one good species into two on fairly trivial grounds. I have been able to look at what constitutes a species from a detached standpoint and notes are included, where relevant, on taxonomic issues.

For the purposes of this book, Europe is taken as all the countries east as far as the Dardanelles, Bosphorus and Black Sea, then north through the Sea of Asov, along the valleys of the Rivers Don and Volga to the Urals, and thence north on longitude 60°E to the Arctic Ocean. The off-lying islands of Iceland, the Faroes and Svalbard to the north, and the Mediterranean islands of the Balearics, Corsica, Sardinia, Sicily and Malta to the south are also included.

Some might disagree with the eastern boundary that has been taken, though the Ural mountain chain has long been accepted as separating Europe from Asia. So too has the Bosphorus separated Europe from Asia Minor. But to go further east and include the truly Asiatic states of Israel, Syria, Iraq, Azerbaijan and Armenia, as did the Food and Agriculture Organisation of the United Nations in its 1971 catalogue, *European Inland Water Fish*, is stretching European bounds too far!

European freshwater fish are in need of being taken seriously by the conservationists and by politicians throughout Europe. For, as the following pages will demonstrate, all is far from well. We are at the turn of the 21st century. Unless action is taken now to conserve European freshwater fish and what little remains of pristine freshwater habitats, by the turn of the 22nd century a quarter of species will have become extinct. I hope that someone reading this book in the year 2100 exclaims, 'Thank goodness they did it!'

MALCOLM GREENHALGH

The Atlantic salmon, king of fish. Its scientific name, Salmo salar, means 'the salmon that leaps'.

The Origins of European Fish Fauna

The last major Pleistocene Ice Age lasted for about 70,000 years and retreated from Europe about 12,000–15,000 years ago. During this Ice Age, fish were excluded from much of northern and upland Europe, for the rivers and lakes, like the land, were frozen solid and covered with snow and ice.

A Swiss headwater stream of the River Danube. When the ice melted 12,000 years ago, species such as the brown trout, grayling, chub and nase colonised here by swimming upstream from the Danube River.

There were at least three and probably five major European Ice Age 'refuges': areas that were not icebound and where freshwater fish managed to survive – southern Iberia, the Po Valley/Lombardy region of northern Italy, the Danube/Black Sea region, southern Greece and the lower reaches of the Rhone. Some more northerly areas, fringing the permanent snow and ice fields, may have retained some fish stocks, but these would have been species that are found today in high Arctic areas including arctic charr, whitefish and perhaps salmon and trout.

During the thousands of years that the European fish stocks were separated in the Pleistocene refuges, many of the closely related modern species evolved. For example, the barbel (see pages 120–25) originated in the Danube refuge, the Iberian and Portuguese barbel in the

Iberian refuge, the Peloponnesian, Thracian and Euboean barbel in Greece, and the Italian and Mediterranean barbel in the Po Valley refuge.

As the climate improved, fish returned northwards and westwards in order to colonise the empty rivers and lakes. It is possible, by comparing the position of the five refuges and the distribution maps of many species, to gain clues about which refuges those species came from, post Ice Age.

Sea-run species

Anadromous and catadromous species were able to colonise from the sea. They penetrated all European rivers, unless there was an impassable barrier, such as a high waterfall, or where an upland lake lacked a connection with the sea. In this way, lampreys, eel, salmon, brown trout, arctic charr, whitefish, smelt, sticklebacks, sea bass, mullets, the freshwater blenny and gobies recolonised freshwater.

Freshwater routes

Many freshwater fish, such as pike, perch and members of the carp family, cannot tolerate full-strength seawater and so they would have spread naturally into regions only via rivers and lakes. Following the great melt, rivers were larger and there was a complex of lakes over much of Europe, which disappeared as the snow and ice finally melted and drained away.

Several great river systems – the Danube, Rhine and Rhone – enabled the spread of fish northwards, through the heart of Europe from the Po, Danube, Rhone and Greek refuges. By contrast, the Iberian refuge fish had no river route into the rest of Europe, their eastward spread being limited by the Pyrenees.

Changing temperature

Many fish species, such as carp and tench, require high summer water temperatures in order to be able to spawn successfully and this has restricted their colonisation of the far north. By contrast, other species, such as salmon and arctic charr, require cool water temperatures for spawning and, as they extended their ranges northwards after the retreat of the Ice Age, their southerly limit moved northwards as water temperatures in southern Europe became too high. The Atlantic salmon, which flourished in rivers flowing into the Mediterranean during maximum glaciation, today has its potential southerly limit in the Tagus River (although subsequent damming and pollution have eradicated salmon from all Portuguese rivers). Similarly the arctic charr: 100 years ago it ran rivers northwards of 62°N; in the 1900s it has retreated northwards and runs only rivers that are north of 64°N.

However, the populations of some fish species have remained in refuge areas where the main populations can no longer be found. The Adriatic salmon, for example, remains in Macedonian rivers that have now been abandoned by Atlantic salmon. In addition to this, some, usually lake populations of northern fish species, survive as 'landlocked' or 'Arctic relict' populations, such as arctic charr and whitefish in lakes in central Europe and the British Isles.

Human influence

Human beings have introduced many species into European waters where they did not naturally occur. This has included spreading fish that had a restricted distribution, usually in eastern Europe, through most of the remainder of the continent, for example catfish, carp and zander. It also includes 20 species that are not endemic in Europe, such as rainbow trout, largemouth bass and mosquito fish.

Present-day distributions have also been affected by human destruction: by pollution, river damming and lake drainage (see pages 16–19).

It is not surprising, therefore, that the closer you get to an Ice Age refuge, the more likely you are to find more species of fish. And, the further you are from a refuge, there will be a higher proportion of fish species that have been introduced by man.

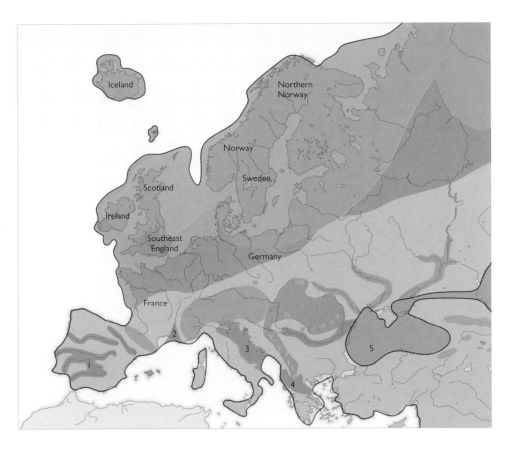

Europe at maximum glaciation about 17,000 years ago. Much of the continent was in the grip of snow and ice and the freshwater fish restricted to Ice Age refuges. It was in these refuges that many of the fish species and subspecies we see today evolved, and from these refuges that fish colonised the rest of Europe after the last Ice Age ended.

River/Country	Indigenous species	Introduced species
River Danube (a refuge)	79	4
Northern Italy (a refuge)	54	8
Spain (a refuge)	41	8
Germany	59	8
France	53	13
Sweden	47	4
Southeast England	42	13
Norway	36	4
Northern Norway	16*	3
Scotland	17	21
Ireland	16*	13
Iceland	6*	perhaps 1–2

All anadromous or catadromous

Key
— Sea level 17,000 years ago
▪ Permanent ice and snow fields
▪ Tundra or tundra-like vegetation
▪ Steppe vegetation
▪ Refuges
  1 Iberian refuge
  2 Rhone refuge
  3 Po refuge
  4 Greek refuge
  5 Danube/Black Sea refuge

River Fish Communities

Most European rivers rise high in mountains. Exceptions include short chalkstreams and other lowland rivers that rise in springs at the foot of relatively low, usually chalk, hills.

High mountain streams: trout zone

The uppermost feeder streams flow turbulently down a steep, usually unstable, boulder river bed. Because of the nature of the bed and, to some extent, the purity of the water, water weeds are absent; the only plant life will be temporary growths of algae on boulders or leaf material washed into the water. Fish foods are dominated by stoneflies and mayflies, although densities are usually low. The fish community is usually dominated by brown trout, although eels and minnows may be present.

Upper river reaches: grayling zone

Several feeder streams eventually join to produce the upper river reaches. Here, in the upper valley, there is more stability: the river flows less turbulently down a shallower bed in which a pattern of pools and connecting riffles is established. In the steeper, shallower riffles the bed often comprises unstable boulders and the flow is turbulent. But in the deep pools the flow tends to be less turbulent and the loose boulders of the

riffle are replaced by shingle and finer gravel. By the time it has flowed here from its mountain source, the water will have accumulated more mineral nutrients and, as well as algae on boulders and shingle, rocks in sheltered corners have thick growths of water-moss. Stoneflies and mayflies usually dominate the insect fish-foods, but midge, blackflies and caddis are present in high densities with increasing populations as one moves downstream. The fish community is dominated by the brown trout and grayling. Eels, minnows and nase may occur and salmon spawn here.

Middle river reaches: barbel or chub zone

The character of the upper river gradually gives way to the middle river reaches. Here the river meanders within the confines of the lower valley, and the pools on the sweeping bends have beds of sand, with fine gravel in the pool necks and tails. The very shallow gradient through the pools results in a steady flow almost completely lacking in turbulence. The gradient is always steeper through the riffles that link pools, and here shingle

High mountain streams: trout zone
The trout zone is found at these altitudes – the brown trout species is dominant.

Upper river reaches: grayling zone
In these parts of a river system, the grayling and trout species are dominant.

usually dominates the bed, with scattered fixed boulders. The banks are often fairly intensively farmed, usually with improved pastures for beef or dairy cattle. This results in more nutrients being washed into the water from fertilisers and animal wastes and there are often lush growths of weed such as water buttercup *Ranunculus*. Stonefly numbers usually decline here and mayflies, caddis, midges and blackflies dominate the insect fish foods; freshwater shrimps and snails are also important foods.

Here the fish community is usually most diverse. Barbel and chub are often dominant together with dace, nase, brown trout, grayling, minnow, pike and eel among the commoner species. Sea lamprey, lampern and shads migrate from the sea to spawn here. Salmon rest in this zone on their upstream migration and some salmon parr may move downstream to feed here.

Lower river reaches: bream zone
The river water completes its journey to the estuary in the lower river reaches. Here the river is no longer hemmed in by a narrow valley, but meanders widely through a broad floodplain of fine fertile silt that makes such excellent farmland that it is usually intensively farmed for arable crops.

Large amounts of fertilisers poured on the land result in high concentrations leaching into the river. In addition industrial and household effluents are often dumped from towns or cities straddling the lower reaches. Although sewage is mostly treated before release, high mineral nutrient levels remain.

Along this part of its course the river is at its least turbulent; the smooth river bed (sand or gravel in deep riffles and silt or mud in the meander pools) does not interrupt the flow. You can see this at the water surface, which is smooth and completely flat, with a little wind ripple – a complete contrast to the white, broken surface far upstream. Sometimes the river here tends to be turbid, but where the water is clear, dense weedbeds cover the bottom. Stoneflies and mayflies are usually missing, with two exceptions where the water is very clean: *Baetis rhodani* and *Caenis*, and caddis, midges, crustaceans and molluscs dominate invertebrate fish-foods, with damselfly nymphs and waterboatmen in the densest weed beds.

Bream, blue bream, roach, bleak, chub, dace, gudgeon and other cyprinids usually dominate the fish community, together with eel, pike, perch and zander. Anadromous species pass through the lower river reaches to spawn farther upstream.

Rivermouth
The estuary carries fresh water into the sea. However, saltwater and freshwater do not immediately mix – they remain separated in many estuaries, the freshwater flowing over the salt. Some freshwater fish, such as grayling, cannot tolerate the slightest brackishness, whereas others, such as trout, zahrte and zeige, move into the estuary to feed. Some saltwater species will move into the estuary to feed, often penetrating freshwater. And lampreys, sturgeon, eels, shads and salmonids move through the estuary at they move between feeding and spawning areas.

Exceptions to the rule
Many smaller rivers do not follow the zone pattern. Often one zone may be missing or, in very short streams, the river may be entirely one zone. The mountain rivers of Norway, for instance, are trout zone throughout. Lowland, spring-formed chalk and limestone streams also do not follow this pattern. The chalk streams of southern England have a mixed fish community that includes eel, pike, perch, three-spined stickleback, miller's thumb and shoals of fast-growing cyprinids: carp, chub, dace, roach, rudd, minnow, bream, silver bream, bleak, barbel, gudgeon and stone loach.

Middle river reaches: barbel or chub zone
The barbel and chub are the dominant species in these parts of the river.

Lower river reaches: bream zone
Although this part of the river is called the bream zone, many cyprinids may share dominance with them.

Lake Fish Communities

Lakes are bodies of still water, and can vary in size from small dew ponds and fenland meres to almost inland seas, such as Ladoga in Russia and Vanern in Sweden, where it is impossible to see across to the other side. They can also vary in depth from 1–2m to over 100m.

One of the most important features of lakes is the productivity of their water, in terms of plant nutrients. Each lake can be put into one of three general categories of productivity.

Oligotrophic lakes

This lake type is found where the concentration of plant nutrients is very small. Plant growth in the margins of the lake is sparse and the density of phytoplankton in the surface layers of open water is extremely low. When there is such little plant life, there are only meagre populations of plant-eating invertebrates, including mayflies and stoneflies, which, in turn, result in tiny populations of slow-growing fish.

Usually found in mountainous areas or in the far north of Europe (Scotland, Iceland and Fenno-Scandinavia), oligotrophic lakes have very little intensive agriculture or urban development situated around them. The fish community usually consists of brown trout, minnow, eel and migratory salmon that spawn in the feeder streams. They often have Ice Age relict fish: one of the three European species of whitefish, smelt or arctic charr. Pike and perch often occur, although they will have been mostly introduced.

Mesotrophic lakes

These lakes are more productive than oligotrophic but not as productive as eutrophic lakes. There will be some agriculture in their catchment and some small towns, but these will add only moderate amounts of nutrients and the lakes remain moderately productive. Many of the great limestone lakes of Ireland, the lowland lakes of Scotland, the vast waters of southern Finland and Sweden, and the shallow lakes of the alpine regions are mesotrophic.

The fish communities in mesotrophic lakes are dominated by fast-growing brown trout, sometimes with Ice Age relict populations of arctic charr or a whitefish species. In eastern Europe burbot are often common. In mainland Europe pike, perch and cyprinids such as roach and bream are sometimes very abundant in this type of lake.

Oligotrophic lake
This type of lake typically has a rocky bed, sparse vegetation, great light penetration and small fish populations.

Light zone

Depth in metres
0 — 2 — 4 — 6 — 8 — 10 — 12 — 14 — 16 — 18 — 20

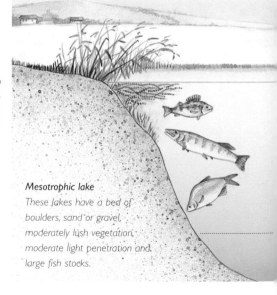

Mesotrophic lake
These lakes have a bed of boulders, sand or gravel, moderately lush vegetation, moderate light penetration and large fish stocks.

Eutrophic lakes

These are the richest and most productive lakes. They are usually found in lowland areas in intensively farmed land and with towns situated around them. High concentrations of nutrients entering the lake result in lush growths of water weed in the margins and vast densities of phytoplankton in the surface layers of the open water. These feed vast populations of invertebrates, but the very clean water-dependent mayflies and stoneflies are usually missing. The invertebrates are food for fast-growing fish. Most of the lakes, meres and ponds of lowland northwest Europe are eutrophic.

The fish community usually includes eels, pike, carp, crucian carp, roach, rudd, bitterling, bream, silver bream, tench, catfish, three-spined stickleback, perch, ruffe and zander. Brown and rainbow trout are sometimes introduced to small eutrophic lakes.

Some lakes are extremely eutrophic: so much so that in winter, when the water is covered by ice, or during a long hot summer oxygen levels fall so low that few fish can survive. Then eels, mudminnows, nine-spined sticklebacks and, in southern European coastal areas where the lakes are slightly brackish, one of the toothcarp species may be the only inhabitants.

Eutrophication

An ever increasing problem in European lakes, eutrophication is especially problematic in lowland areas. Eutrophication occurs when the nutrients entering a lake are increased, usually as a result of an increasing intensity of agriculture or from sewage outfalls into the lake. It results in oligotrophic lakes becoming mesotrophic, and mesotrophic becoming eutrophic. And it often results in changes in the fish community: salmonids tend to decline and cyprinids increase. Ireland's Lough Derravargh, for example, was a famous mesotrophic lake up until about 1950, with a big population of fast growing trout. By 1990 eutrophication, through leaching of wastes from pig and dairy farms, had wiped out the trout, and cyprinids now dominate the fish community.

Fish zones in lakes

Sunlight can only penetrate so far into a lake as phytoplankton and chemicals dissolved in water absorb light as it passes through. The more phytoplankton and chemicals in the water, the shallower light can penetrate. In summer, sunlight may reach a maximum depth of 1–2m in eutrophic lakes, 2–6m in mesotrophic lakes, and 6–20m or more in oligotrophic lakes.

Pond weeds, rooted in the bottom of lakes, need sunlight and so they are found only in water shallow enough for light to reach the bottom. They live in a shallow water light zone around lake margins, around offshore islands and over reefs. Weedbeds harbour large populations of invertebrates and these attract the fish. This shallow zone is highly productive in a mesotrophic lake: if productivity on the lake bed in water up to 5m deep equals 100 units per square metre, in water 5–10m deep, productivity will equal 10 units per square metre, and in water deeper than 10m only one unit per square metre. Fish that usually feed on the bottom will therefore be concentrated in the shallow water light zone.

The deeper, open water light zone, however, is also productive. Enormous populations of phytoplankton develop from mid-spring to autumn in the sunlit surface layer and are eaten by a population explosion of zooplankton (mostly tiny crustaceans, but also phantom-fly larvae). The fish filter out the zooplankton using their gill rakers: trout, charr, whitefish and smaller cyprinids all filter-feed on zooplankton. And pike and big 'ferox' trout lie in wait in the dim light at the bottom of the open water light zone in order to ambush the shoals of filter-feeders.

Eutrophic lake
These lakes have a sand or mud bed, luxuriant plant life, a very shallow light zone and a huge fish population.

Canal and Drain Fish Communities

Man-made waterways are used as a means of transport and for draining water from large tracts of low-lying marshy land. Most were excavated over 100 years ago so today they are often quite mature bodies of freshwater that resemble very slow-moving rivers.

Canals

Most canals are long with a series of locks to carry the canal over high ground and, sometimes, an entrance via a lock into a river estuary shipping channel. As boats open and close locks, water moves downhill through the system so that the canal can look like a very slow-flowing river. Canal water tends to be rich in plant nutrients, which are leached from surrounding farmland or urban effluents. In industrial areas factories often extract water from canals to use for cooling purposes, and return it as hot water. This results in rich conditions, which in summer causes weed growths that are so lush that they must be cut back in some canals in order to keep the waterway open. In canals elsewhere the water tends to be so turbid that little sunlight reaches the bottom and rooted water weeds are not able to grow.

A wet margin close to the bank, where the bank is not concreted, usually has a lush growth of reed, pond-sedge or other marginal plants. This is the major fish spawning area in spring when the canal water is at a high level. Even pike and carp will spawn here in less than 50cm of water, although if water levels fall before fry are capable of swimming away, there is a danger that all the spawn may be lost.

A narrow strip of shallow water lies alongside the wet margin. In clear-water canals, this area will usually be made up of a luxuriant mass of Canadian pondweed or sometimes one of the Potamogeton pondweeds. This is both a spawning area and the main nursery area for fish. Carp and tench may move in to feed on the bottom of the canal at night, and perch will hunt fry here. Sticklebacks and bitterling have been known to live here permanently.

Canals

Canals are often linear aquatic wildlife corridors, carrying water, plants, insects, molluscs and amphibians, as well as fish, into European cities and intensely farmed areas. Canals are also the last refuge for aquatic wildlife species in the many lowland fens, lakes and meres that have been drained in the last 250 years.

A deep water boat channel is home to shoals of smaller species, such as roach. They concentrate along the steep drop-off from shallow water, while larger carp, bream, tench, zander and pike will be found mostly in deep water.

Drains

Usually long, straight waterways, drains have a network of side branches that are often arranged in a herringbone or rectangular pattern over large blocks of flat farmland. Land-drains pour water, which often has a high fertiliser content from surrounding rich arable farmland, into the drain and, whenever the water table nears the surface of the surrounding land, surplus is pumped away into rivers or the sea.

During periods of wet weather, usually autumn and early spring, the main drain may have a strong flow; during summer droughts there may be little flow and water may be pumped from the drain to irrigate surrounding farmland. In some drains, especially side-drains, the water may be so clear that rooted water weeds grow prolifically along the bottom. However most drains are too turbid for weed growth.

Drains usually contain a shallow, U-shaped cross section, which has extremely narrow, wet margins and shallows. Shoals of smaller cyprinids tend to haunt the margins where they are harried by predators, such as pike, perch and zander, while larger bottom-feeders such as carp, bream and tench prefer to seek out the muddy-bottomed depths of the drain.

Drains almost always, and canals often, are stark, exposed waters and any cover or other 'feature' always attracts fish. The branches of an overhanging tree, a patch of reedbed or an abandoned barge will provide an ambush lie where pike or perch can await the arrival of a shoal of roach or small 'skimmer' bream. Predators such as pike will often lie downstream of a canal lock, waiting for the next boat to release a surge of water containing lesser fish. Large shoals of smaller cyprinids often congregate where a canal widens in a marina or basin, or where a side-drain joins the main drain, and the predator fish lurk close by.

Canal and drain fish

Fish communities that live in canals and drains depend, to a certain extent, on what was put in the waterways after they were built, although some fish may have colonised from inflowing streams. Most canals and drains are unable to support populations of very clean-water fish, such as brown trout and grayling, because of their eutrophic nature and even if these fish species were able to survive in the water they would be unable to breed because there are no suitable 'spawning gravels'.

The following species are commonly found in both canals and drains: pike, eels (they reach canals and drains by crossing over wet farmland during the night), carp, crucian carp, roach, rudd, bitterling (only in canals or drains that contain swan mussels), bream, silver bream, tench, three-spined stickleback, perch, ruffe and zander. In urban areas, where warm water is sometimes pumped into canals, goldfish and tropical fish such as guppies have been known to thrive. In recent

A canal rich in floating algae and weed produces large numbers of invertebrates and huge populations of fast-growing fish.

years, American sunfish species (black and brown bullheads and pumpkinseed) have been released into canals.

Habitat conservation

Although canals and drains were originally built for practical purposes, they should also be managed and maintained as aquatic wildlife reserves. In addition to the fish species that are now threatened, many aquatic plants and other animals have lost habitat in industrialised Europe over the course of the past 150 years. If one bank and one margin were left undredged and unmanicured along all Europe's canals and drains, narrow reedbeds and willow carr would be able to flourish and provide havens for many of the water and waterside species that we have almost exterminated by our actions.

Conservation Issues

One afternoon in April 1993 a tanker holding 180,000 litres of ammonium hydroxide tipped over, spilling its entire contents into a small stream of the River Eden, England. The emergency services and the Environment Agency, the government body responsible for controlling pollution in England and Wales, were summoned and they prevented the noxious chemical reaching the main river. But, as night fell, the Environment Agency took down the emergency dam and went home.
The incident was reported to no one in the valley.

By the following morning the chemical had swept through 5km of the main river and destroyed the entire fish stock. Brown trout, grayling, brook lampreys, chub and minnow littered the river bed in their thousands. Eel corpses were everywhere, including over 40m from the river in fields where they had crawled to escape the burning effects of ammonia on their gills. Three years' production of salmon died: the emerging fry from the 1992 spawning, the parr from the 1991 spawning that would have gone to sea a few weeks later, and the four-year-old adult salmon that had recently run the river and would have spawned later that year.

The pollution moved farther downstream and eventually destroyed all the fish for about 30km. That year the kingfishers, which would have bred here, had to leave. The grey herons, nesting in a wood close by, raised an average of 0.3 young per pair: in 1982 they had reared an average of 2.3. This one-off 'accident' failed to make national TV and radio news, and featured as one small paragraph on the inside pages of some national newspapers. Why? Because fish are 'unattractive'

animals. Because fish are loved only by anglers who spend their time trying to catch them. Had the fish that died been grey seals, dolphins or just about any bird species they would have made the front page headlines and national news bulletins.

Unfortunately wildlife conservation in the British Isles and much of Europe is a media-manipulated, fundraising affair that promotes and exploits cuddly, furry mammals or spectacular birds. Funds flow in after every announcement that such and such a species is 'endangered'. In Britain, birds of prey such as ospreys, hen harriers, golden eagles, peregrines and red kites are said to be endangered, yet there are many more of these birds of prey now than there have been for at least 100 years, and none is threatened with extinction. So what does endangered mean? As far as its meaning in this book is concerned, for the term features all too often, endangered means likely to become extinct by the year 2050 (and many earlier than that) unless steps are taken to prevent it. And not simply extinct in one country, extinct as a world species. Of the 174 fish species described in this book, 22 are non-native and 152 native. Of the native fish, at least 42 species (27 per cent) are endangered.

There are therefore two chief problems faced by any fish conservationist. First, wildlife organisations tend to ignore fish. The cause of fish is taken up by anglers who, because they catch fish, are also ignored and often railed against by naturalists. Second, because of the wildlife lobby, the wildlife departments at TV companies also tend to ignore fish – fish just don't make good airtime. As a result, fish stocks are collapsing without the public, including naturalists, being aware of it.

But why should we conserve every species of European freshwater fish? Does it really matter if one becomes extinct? After all, most of them are

An environmental tragedy that is so often ignored by conservation organisations.

of no economic importance. Surely, nothing is lost if one species disappears. I could attempt to produce economic reasons for conserving all fish species. Other fish-eating animals, such as herons and otters, depend on the survival of fish. Fish are potentially important sources of food for humans. The very rare and most threatened species might hold genes that, in the future, could solve a major world health or food problem and, by allowing these genes to become extinct, you lose the potential answers to lots of potential problems. But I think that the real reason is deeper and teaches us a lot about ourselves. To allow any species to become extinct is a crime against creation or against the history and evolution of life. And a society of European nations that does not act to prevent the loss of any plant or animal species cannot call itself civilised.

Over-fishing

Although over-fishing may greatly reduce a fish population, there is no instance of any European freshwater fish population becoming endangered through over-fishing by rod-and-line anglers. Indeed, it would not be in the anglers' interests for this to happen and anglers make sure that it does not. In fact, the majority of anglers do far more for freshwater wildlife conservation in general than do non-angling conservation bodies. Anglers monitor and conserve freshwater habitats rigorously.

- They improve habitats, including tree and shrub planting at the waterside and carry out river bank and river pool repair following any damage. Where an angling association properly manages a river or small lake, the outcome is a wildlife haven.
- Anglers have added to freshwater habitats. They buy flooded sand and gravel pits that would otherwise be used as land-fill sites.
- They monitor water quality and ring alarm bells when a problem emerges.
- Anglers pay for hatcheries that can be used to bolster wild fish stocks. Without this work, two species – the marbled trout and the huchen – would be on the point of extinction now.
- They fund and promote the conservation of anadromous species in the marine stage of their lives. If it wasn't for anglers, Atlantic salmon would

still be netted uncontrollably in the Atlantic and inshore waters, despite the reluctance of British and Irish governments, who still allow their offshore net fisheries to take too many salmon. Without this lobby the fact that salmon farming destroys wild sea trout stocks would never have been admitted by government fishery scientists. And without the anglers' lobby, dams across rivers would not have 'passes' for anadromous fish.

Accidental pollution

Pollution can be a constant, on-going problem, or an 'accidental' one-off spillage. One-off spillages may happen by 'accident', but they happen all too often. The tap left open that destroys over 35km of river with creosote; the farm slurry pit that leaks into the river; the sewage works that releases untreated sewage/acid/caustic fluids into a river when the wrong valve is inadvertently opened; the cyanide that escapes from a factory that makes aircraft engines; the milk processing plant that accidentally washes its waste into the river and kills all the fish for more than 45km. Prosecutions occur, but penalties are too often a miserable token.

The conservation of European rivers and lakes is in the hands of anglers, without whom we would have far less water clean enough for fish and other wildlife.

Long-term pollution

During the Industrial Revolution the banks of the lower reaches of most large European rivers were developed as major cities and the river was used as a repository for waste. By the middle of the 20th century, estuaries of rivers such as the Rhine and Thames were so filthy that little could live there, and no anadromous fish would pass through. In recent years a positive effort has been made by governments to have cleaner rivers, and salmon have now returned to the Thames and Rhine. However, there are now other forms of pollution. The European Union (EU) subsidises farmers to throw huge quantities of chemical fertilisers – containing the three plant growth elements nitrogen, phosphorus and potassium (NPK) – onto their fields. A large proportion of these chemicals leach into water courses and eventually into rivers and lakes where, in spring, the chemicals encourage the growth of an algae, *Cladophora*, which clothes the river beds and lake margins. During hot summer nights, the *Cladophora* deoxygenates the water and fish-food species, such as stoneflies and mayflies, which need high oxygen levels are killed. In prolonged, extremely hot summers, oxygen levels may fall so low that trout and salmon parr are killed. And when the *Cladophora* dies and decomposes in the autumn, particles sink into the gravel nests of salmon and trout and suffocate the eggs that lie there.

Fertiliser regulation

The use of NPK fertilisers ought to be far more tightly regulated than it is at present. Currently the EU Common Agricultural Policy (CAP) results in excessive cereal and dairy production and both rely on high quantities of NPK fertilisers. The excess food is stored, destroyed or sold to non-EU countries at less than the cost of production. By reducing the NPK treatment on farmland, food production and water pollution would both be reduced. Farmers would still receive the same income from CAP grants, the EU would have all the food it needed without wasting money on storage and fertiliser subsidies. At the same time, quite precise annual soil testing should be used to calculate exactly what amounts of NPK fertlisers are needed on a particular field. It is too easy to add high quantities of subsidised fertliser and ignore the fact that all the excess will end up in waterways.

Excessive fertiliser use is a problem in itself, but it also contributes to the general trend of eutrophication in freshwater habitats. The mineral nutrient level in the water increases, which in turn increases the amount of plant growth, which in turn provides more food for invertebrates. You might expect that eutrophication could be beneficial, increasing the growth rate of fish. To some extent it can be, but only up to a point. If plant growth is increased, more dead plant material will decay, and oxygen levels will therefore fall. The more plants there are, the greater that fall will be.

Sewage effluent

Modern sewage works discharge effluent that lacks the organic component that old sewage works released; instead the clear fluid is a solution of chemicals including plant nutrients. The chemical concentration in this effluent is high because of the massive use of detergents. Higher concentrations of livestock on modern farms also contribute to eutrophication. The chemicals in their urine and faeces eventually find their way into rivers and lakes from the fields.

England's only landlocked smelt population, at Rostherne Mere, was lost in the 1920s because of eutrophication; so too were pollan stocks in half the European lakes (Loughs Ree and Derg) where this Ice Age relict species occurred. The vendace population of Castle Loch vanished in the 1910s and Mill Loch in the 1970s through eutrophication and the burbot became extinct in England in the 1970s. The problem continues, and will result in further local losses of clean water fish – charr and whitefish seem especially vulnerable – unless 'scrubbers' (contraptions that can remove the worst nutrient chemicals) are fitted to sewage works and an alternative strategy is employed in the treatment of farm livestock. Again, the problem is money and a political will to do something about it.

Pesticide pollution

Although the use of organo-halide pesticides, which caused so much damage to wildlife in the 1950–60s, has been banned, pesticides continue to be a major problem in some areas. For example, new pyrethoid pesticides were introduced in 1996 to control sheep ticks on hill farms throughout sheep-rearing regions of the EU. The pesticides kill only insects and are not harmful to other forms of wildlife or to farmers. However, if a sheep that has recently been dipped in pyrethoids walks through a small stream, a few drops dripping from its fleece will kill all the insect fish foods over a considerable distance downstream. In northern England, all the aquatic insects living in an 11km stretch of the upper Ribble and 9km stretch of the Wharfe were destroyed in two incidents. The trout and grayling in these rivers had no food and they starved to death. There is a pyrethroid pellet that can be injected under a sheep's skin, which removes all risk to water courses, but farmers will

A pool choked with blanketweed, an alga that thrives in water polluted with agricultural fertilisers. Such a 'bloom' will kill most freshwater fish.

not use it. The reason is that a sheep that has been treated by pellets cannot go to market for 30 days after treatment . . .

Acidification

Power stations in England, Germany and Poland produce huge quantities of nitric and sulphuric acid and release them as smoke into the atmosphere. Eventually these chemicals return to earth as 'acid rain', reducing the pH of rivers and lakes from 6.5–7.5 to 4.5–5.5, which is a hundredfold increase in acidity. Furthermore, the now acidic water, flowing through coniferous forests especially, produces ideal conditions for the release of poisonous aluminium salts from the soil. These salts are insoluble at normal, higher pHs. The consequence is death of the fish in that water.

Acid rain does not fall where it is made; it is carried by the wind and falls on mountainous areas – in southern Scandinavia, Scotland and

Wales – where most people will never see its effects. But it has already sterilised several lakes and rivers in these regions, destroying many fish populations. There is a solution: power stations could instal 'scrubbers' to remove acidic gases before smoke is released, but, again, this is deemed too expensive.

River damming

The river dam, built to produce hydroelectric power and collect freshwater, has had more impact on fish stocks than any other form of pollution. It destroys the streamy habitat and prevents fish from moving through the river between spawning and feeding areas. On some salmon rivers, dams have 'fish passes' that allow fish to move through, although never as freely as they would be able to without the dam. Other species of fish, which have little or no commercial value, have no such provision.

In many rivers, whole populations of fish have been exterminated as a result of dam construction – sea lamprey, lampern, sturgeon, allis shad, twaite shad, Atlantic salmon, sea trout, sea-run arctic charr, zahrte and zeige (in Baltic rivers), soufie, southern barbel and asp. Throughout the whole of Europe, the following species have become endangered primarily as a consequence of the building of river dams – huchen, Adriatic salmon, barbel-gudgeon, Kessler's gudgeon, schraetzer, asprete, zingel, asper and striped ruffe.

Wetland drainage

Over the course of the last century, many of Europe's freshwater marshes, bogs and fens were drained. This drainage continues today and it is likely that, by the end of the 21st century, there will be none of this fascinating habitat left outside nature reserves. Fish populations including the swamp minnow, European mudminnow and moderlieschen are declining alarmingly as a result of drainage, which, together with the use of

A dam on a Balkan river: dams like this, which prevent fish passing freely between feeding and spawning grounds, are one of the greatest threats to European fish.

pesticides and the introduction of mosquito fish, is also contributing to the demise of the toothcarp species.

Alien fish

Many wild European fish populations have been damaged by the introduction of non-native fish. American rainbow trout is one of the worst species: it will devour the eggs and fry of native fish and harry adult native fish from any pool it wishes to use. This species was a primary cause of the marbled trout almost becoming extinct. Rainbow trout should never again be released in any wild river or lake. They should be stocked only into artificial lakes from which they cannot escape.

Similarly the mosquito fish, which was introduced to pools along the Mediterranean coast to control the mosquito population: it has contributed to the collapse of Valencia toothcarp in some areas. And the ruffe, which was put into lakes such as Loch Lomond, threatens the future of the Ice Age relict population of powan. Stocking any wild river or lake with fish species that do not naturally occur there is a form of pollution and European law should treat it as such.

Our wild European fish have survived some 10,000 years since the end of the last Ice Age and over 100 years of threats posed by industrialised man. To risk their survival by introducing any non-native fish into a wild river or lake should be considered an act of gross negligence. It is our responsibility – the EU, national and local governments, wildlife and conservation organisations, and angling bodies – to fight hard to protect our clean rivers, lakes and inshore waters and their natural wild fish stocks.

Identifying Fish

The certain identification of a fish is, in some cases, quite easy. It would be difficult, for example, to mistake pike or perch for any other species. However, it is not so easy in other cases, particularly for species in larger families, such as the salmonids and cyprinids, where diagnostic differences between species are often quite subtle.

Colour and size are often too variable in closely related species to be a safe guide, although they do provide extra clues for identification. It is much better, though, to use obvious physical features that can be noted, counted or measured, such as the presence and arrangement of fins and the shape and size of the mouth.

Length

The length of the fish is taken as a straight line from the tip of the snout to the base of the tail fin fork and is given in centimetres, sometimes metres. Length of head, snout, eye diameter and body depth are usually given as a comparison with another measurement, eg, snout = twice eye diameter; maximum depth = half body length.

Rays and spines

Fins are supported by segmented rays, which may either be branched or unbranched. The number of segmented rays, especially in the case of the dorsal and anal fins, is often a critical identification feature and these ray counts are given in Arabic numerals. In some cyprinids the first one to three rays may sometimes form hard, serrated or toothed spines. A note is given if this is the case. Fins may also be supported by spines: often there are some very soft, very fine, unsegmented 'spines' in front of fins supported by rays. I have ignored these here and taken spines to mean hard, smooth, often sharp structures that are easy to see and count. The number of smooth, sharp spines is usually given in Roman numerals. For example, in the perch: anal II + 8–10 indicates that the anal fin has two sharp spines in front of eight to 10 segmented rays.

Fin position

Some fish species, such as salmonids, have a second dorsal fin that does not have any rays or spines and is known as the adipose (or fatty) fin.

General fish structure (Humpback salmon)

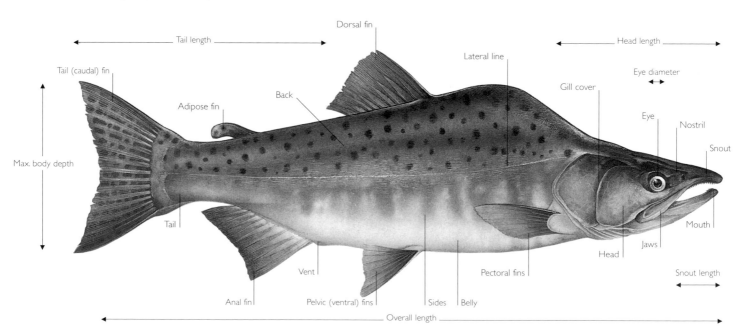

Rays and spines Sharp spine   Branched segmented ray

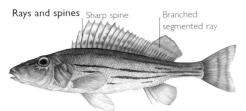

Striped ruffe
The front part of the striped ruffe's dorsal fin is supported by spines and the rear part is supported by branched segmented rays.

Fin position

Adriatic salmon
The dorsal fin base of this fish species is situated in front of pelvic fin base.

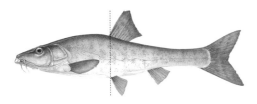

Barbel-gudgeon
The dorsal fin base of this fish species is level with the pelvic fin base.

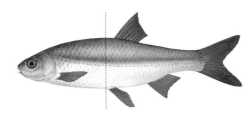

Escalo roach
The dorsal fin base of this fish species is situated slightly to the rear of the pelvic fin.

The positions of fins in relation to the others, most usually the position of the dorsal fin in relation to the pelvic fin, are sometimes important in accurate identification. Take careful note of whether the front of the base of the dorsal fin is in front of, level with, or behind the front of the base of the anal fin.

Mouth and jaws

The shape and precise position of the mouth and jaws of a fish are often very important in making an accurate identification. The mouth can be various different shapes: superior, level, inferior or underslung, and it may sometimes carry barbels – how many are there and how long are they? The jaws may extend back as far as the eye or sometimes beyond the rear of the eye.

Scale counts

These are often important and are given for most fish species as the number of scales that are found along the lateral line from the gill opening to the base of the tail fin. If there is no lateral line, the line is broken or the line curves widely, count the number of scales in a straight line along the side of the body. An adipose count is also given in salmonids; this refers to the number of scales in a line from the lateral line to the adipose fin.

Gills

In this book, I have attempted to give identification characteristics that do not require you actually to kill the fish, so I have excluded physical features such as the number of vertebrae and the colour of the peritoneum. However, in some species it is only possible to make an exact identification by examining parts of the anatomy of a dead fish. The number of gill rakers that are found on the first gill arch is one characteristic and can be diagnostic.

To count gill rakers, remove the gill cover, which will reveal the first gill arch. Carefully cut the gill arch at the dorsal and ventral points of attachment. The long, bright red gill filaments are the fish's respiratory organs, the shorter spiky structures that are found on the inside of the arch are the gill rakers.

Gills

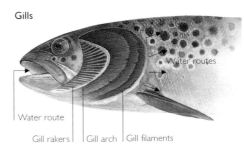

Water route

Gill rakers   Gill arch   Gill filaments

Trout
The gills are the respiratory organs and can help fish identification.

Mouth and jaws

Vendace
Slightly upturned superior mouth extends back to front of eye.

Grayling
Underside mouth: snout extends beyond lower jaw.

Brown trout
Level of mouth extends to beyond rear of eye.

Identifying Cyprinids

Cyprinids are toothless in that they have no true teeth in the mouth. However, they do have structures resembling teeth in the throat that are really bony extensions to the lower pharyngeal bone of the fifth gill arch. These are called pharyngeal teeth. When a cyprinid takes in an item of food, it passes it to the back of the throat and crushes it with these pharyngeal teeth.

I once caught a 2kg chub and, noticing the tail of a small fish stuck in its throat, tried to extract the little fish by sticking my forefinger far down to dislodge it. I felt a muscular contraction and then agony!

The structure and number of pharyngeal teeth is usually fairly constant within one genus or species, but it often varies from one genus or species to the next. They can therefore be used to identify a specimen with a high degree of accuracy when other characteristics leave identification open to doubt. Pharyngeal teeth are also useful if you need to identify a large fish that might be a hybrid, such as a large roach that might be a roach × bream. The only problem is that you have to kill a fish in order to examine its pharyngeal teeth so do this only when necessary.

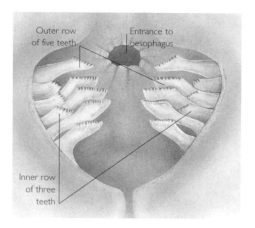

The pharyngeal teeth of the rudd (5+3 : 3+5) seen looking back from the front of the mouth.

Crucian carp
Pharyngeal teeth 4 : 4

Pharyngeal teeth situated inside the throat

How to extract pharyngeal teeth

Kill the fish quickly and take it home. You can store it in a deep-freeze, but do not put it in pickling solution as this tends to erode the pharyngeal teeth.

1. Carefully remove the gill cover without damaging the gills.
2. Remove each gill by severing the gill arches at the bottom and top.
3. The slender pharyngeal bones (one to either side of the throat) are now exposed. Remove these carefully by severing the bones at the top and bottom.
4. Drop the bones/teeth into hot water and leave them there to soak for several minutes; then clean and remove the soft tissues gently using a fine brush.
5. Label each bone by tying on a piece of card that gives all relevant details of species, sex, size (length and weight), date and where you found the fish. Store the teeth or send them to a natural history museum.

Examination and recording

The pharyngeal teeth will be long, relatively slender protuberances. Try to note the following features:
- Count the number of rows of teeth (1, 2 or 3). Check carefully as teeth on the inner row are often smaller and easily overlooked.
- Count the number of teeth in each row. Check closely as sometimes teeth may be broken (look for a stump).
- Record the teeth as follows: $x1+y1+z1 : z2+y2+x2$.
x = number in outer row, y = number in middle row, z = number in inner row (assuming there are 3 rows), 1 = the right-hand side pharyngeal teeth, 2 = the left-hand side pharyngeal teeth. Check both sides as in some species the number, usually in the first row, may be different.
- Examine the teeth with a ×6–10 lens. Look at their shape and general structure. Are the teeth hooked at the tip? Have they flat grinding edges? Have they ridge-like serrations? Compare your findings to the following table.

Common name	Pharyngeal teeth no.	Pharyngeal teeth description
Three rows of pharyngeal teeth		
carp	$3+1+1 : 1+1+3$	flattened surface barbel
barbel	$5+3+2 : 2+3+5$	pointed with hooked tips
Two rows of pharyngeal teeth		
silver bream	$5+2 : 2+5$	flattened with weak hook
schneider	$4 \text{ (or 5)}+2 : 2+4 \text{ (or 5)}$	slender with slight serrations at tip
bleak	$5+2 : 2+5$	serrated close to tip and hooked
asp	$5+3 : 3+5$	smooth, with slight hook
gudgeon	$5+3 \text{ (or 2)} : 2 \text{ (or 3)}+5$	pointed with weak hooks
white-finned gudgeon	$5+3 : 3+5$	pointed and slightly hooked
grass carp	$2+4 \text{ (or 5)} : 4 \text{ (or 5)}+2$	flattened, with folded sides and groove on grinding surface
dace	$5+2 \text{ (rarely 3)} : 2 \text{ (rarely 3)}+5$	smooth with hooked tips
Balkan dace	$5+2 : 2+5$	slender and smooth
ide	$5+3 : 3+5$	smooth, pointed; may have slight hook at tip
chub	$5+2 : 2+5$	smooth or weakly serrated, hooked tip
soufie	$4 \text{ (or 5)}+2 : 2+4 \text{ (or 5)}$	very slender, slight serrations
zeige	$5+2 : 2+5$	slender, slight hook at tip
minnow	$5+2 : 2+5$	very slender
swamp minnow	$5+2 : 2+5$	very slender and fragile
rudd	$5+3 : 3+5$	with ridge-like serrations
One row of pharyngeal teeth		
crucian carp	$4 : 4$	smooth, flattened tips
gibel/goldfish	$4 : 4$	smooth, slender
tench	$4 \text{ (or 5)} : 4 \text{ (or 5)}$	tips often broader than base
bream	$5 : 5$	flattened along sides
Danube bream	$5 : 5$	flattened
blue bream	$5 : 5$	flattened
zahrte	$5 : 5$	flattened and knife-like
nase	$6 : 6$	narrow and dagger-like
southwest European nase	$5 : 5$	flattened and knife-like
minnow nase	$5 : 5$	slender and slightly flattened
moderlieschen	$4 \text{ (or 5)} : 4 \text{ (or 5)}$	very fine
bitterling	$5 : 5$	very fine
roach	usually $5 : 5$ (occasionally 6)	variable; some may be hooked or have a ridge running down the length
escalo roach	$5 : 5$	slender and slightly flattened
Danube roach	$5 : 5$	slender and slightly flattened

Sea Lamprey *Petromyzon marinus*

The largest of the European lampreys, the sea lamprey is a primitive fish that superficially resembles the eel. Although sea lampreys are born and die in freshwater, they spend part of their lives in the sea.

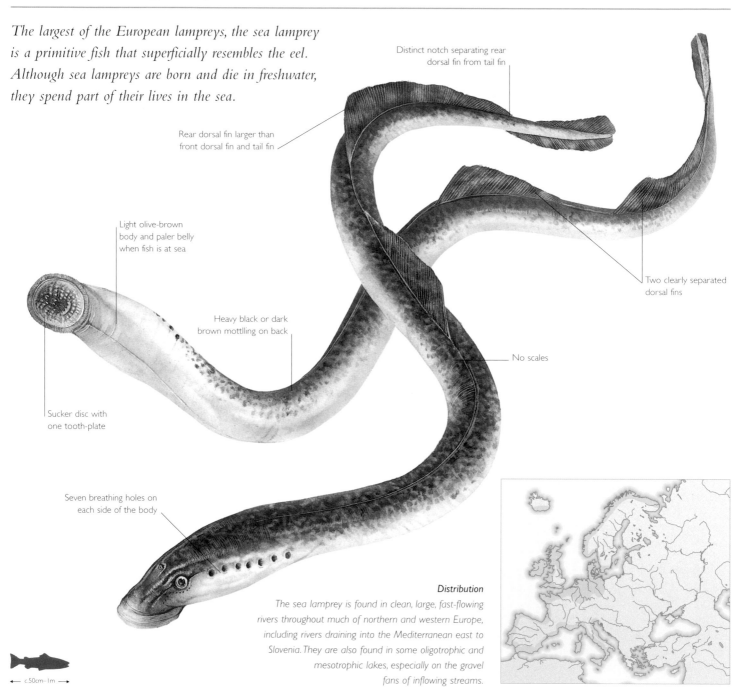

Distinct notch separating rear dorsal fin from tail fin

Rear dorsal fin larger than front dorsal fin and tail fin

Light olive-brown body and paler belly when fish is at sea

Heavy black or dark brown mottlling on back

Two clearly separated dorsal fins

No scales

Sucker disc with one tooth-plate

Seven breathing holes on each side of the body

c.50cm–1m

Distribution
The sea lamprey is found in clean, large, fast-flowing rivers throughout much of northern and western Europe, including rivers draining into the Mediterranean east to Slovenia. They are also found in some oligotrophic and mesotrophic lakes, especially on the gravel fans of inflowing streams.

Like all lampreys, the sea lamprey lacks scales, paired fins, fin rays and spines and gill covers. It usually exceeds 50cm in length and 1kg in weight. The body is long and round in cross section, except towards the rear, where the tail is laterally flattened. Its large sucker disc is surrounded by fimbriae, fringe-like extensions of the skin, and has a large number of small teeth, larger sharp teeth around the front of the mouth, and a tooth-plate with seven to nine large, pointed cusps. When closed the mouth is a slit, but when open it reveals large lingual teeth.

The sexes are identical except for a ridge that develops along the back of the male as he makes his spawning run, and a fold of skin that develops just behind the vent in females. As spawning time approaches the body background colour becomes brighter with a yellow or orange hue.

Breeding behaviour and life cycle

Adult sea lampreys migrate back to the river during early May and June, and gather on suitable spawning areas: extensive gravel beds in streamy, well-oxygenated riffles, usually 1–2m deep. Soon after arriving, in late May, June or July, the male uses his sucker disc to excavate a shallow trough in the gravel, up to 5cm deep. The male then attaches to a female with his sucker disc and leads her to the trough. They lie together, the female sheds her eggs and the male fertilises them. The eggs are then covered, probably by the female. Adult sea lampreys die after spawning, when they are most often seen lying dead on the river bed.

Each female produces about 250,000, 1.2mm-diameter eggs, which are white when laid but fade to a drab, light yellow-brown. These hatch within 10 to 20 days and the 9–11mm larval lampreys, known as ammocoetes, crawl from the nest. They cannot swim against the current; instead they drift downstream to slower, deeper pools where they burrow into gravel, sand and silt on the bed to feed on microscopic algae and bacteria.

The ammocoetes are blind, lack a sucker disc and are a drab grey or blue-grey on the back, and white on the belly; some have been found lacking any pigmentation at all. Growth is very slow: larval sea lampreys may remain in their larval stage for up to five years and even then are only 15–20cm long. In late summer and autumn, they slowly metamorphose into the adult form, but with a grey-blue back and white belly coloration, and head off to sea where they feed and grow. Initially they feed in the estuary and swim slowly through inshore waters before moving to deeper water as far away as the edge of the continental shelf. They stop feeding when they make their spawning run back to the river.

Food and feeding behaviour

Ammocoetes eat algae, especially desmids and diatoms, protozoans, bacteria and particles of organic detritus that they find in the sediments surrounding their burrows. These enter the mouth and are carried in strands of mucus into the gut via conveyor belt-like bands of fine cilia.

When they reach saltwater as adults, they feed by attaching themselves to fish with their sucker discs. They then cut into their hosts' flesh with their rasping teeth, secrete an anticoagulant and suck up blood and digested tissues. Their main hosts are cod, herring and haddock; salmon are occasionally caught bearing the circular, gaping wound made by sea lampreys. They have also been seen on basking sharks and killer whales.

The line of breathing holes along the side and the oral disc separate lampreys from all other fish.

Growth and longevity

During the four to five years as ammocoetes in the river, growth is slow, but accelerates rapidly once sea lampreys become adults and feed on other fish at sea. After one or two years at sea, they reach 50–60cm long. Some sea lampreys return to spawn at this age and size, but others may remain at sea for another one to three years and grow to a maximum length of about 1m.

Conservation status of sea lamprey

Where the spawning rivers, including estuaries, through which sea lampreys must pass twice during their life cycle, remain clean, and if there are no impassable dams or weirs on the river, sea lamprey populations thrive. However, this species is often overlooked because the ammocoete stage remains buried in the river bed, out of sight. Many European rivers have lost their sea lamprey stocks because of pollution and/or river damming, which prevents adult lampreys reaching spawning areas.

Lampern (or River Lamprey) *Lampetra fluviatilis*

Like the sea lamprey, the lampern is an eel-like fish that lacks jaws and instead has a sucker disc with which it feeds as a parasite on other fish. Born in freshwater, it spends part of its life feeding and growing at sea.

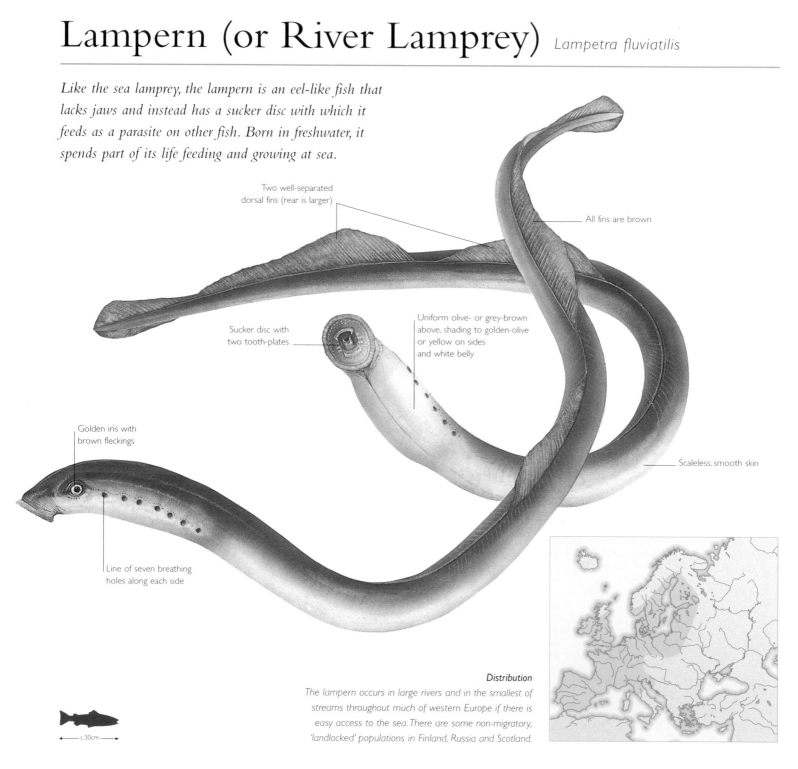

Two well-separated dorsal fins (rear is larger)

All fins are brown

Sucker disc with two tooth-plates

Uniform olive- or grey-brown above, shading to golden-olive or yellow on sides and white belly

Golden iris with brown fleckings

Scaleless, smooth skin

Line of seven breathing holes along each side

c.30cm

Distribution

The lampern occurs in large rivers and in the smallest of streams throughout much of western Europe if there is easy access to the sea. There are some non-migratory, 'landlocked' populations in Finland, Russia and Scotland.

The lampern has scaleless, smooth skin, and, instead of a gill cover, has a line of seven breathing holes extending backwards from just behind the eye on each side of the elongated cylindrical body. It is smaller than the sea lamprey. There are fewer small teeth in the sucker disc, but two tooth-plates, the front one of which has two blunt cusps, and the rear has seven to 10 pointed cusps. There is also a lingual tooth-plate, which has a long, pointed central cusp and tiny cusps on either side.

There are no paired fins; instead the lampern has two dorsal fins that are well separated. The rear dorsal is the larger and connects with the small tail fin. The lampern is often mistaken for the eel (see pages 42–43).

Breeding behaviour and life cycle

Adult lamperns migrate from the sea to rivers mainly from August to November, usually when the river is falling after a spate; some are reported to return in early spring. They do not feed on their return to freshwater; instead the gut degenerates, the fins enlarge slightly, the body shortens and egg and sperm maturation occurs.

Spawning occurs from April to June. The female attaches onto a boulder and lashes at the river bed with her tail to excavate a shallow nest. This lashing may cause her to release pheromones that attract males. If one male lampern arrives, he attaches himself to the female's head with his sucker disc, twines his body around hers, and eggs and sperm are released simultaneously. If several males arrive, the female sheds her eggs and all the males their sperm ensuring a high fertilisation rate. After mating, the female covers the fertilised eggs with gravel. All lamperns die after mating.

Each female lays 30,000–40,000, 1mm-diameter, cream coloured eggs. These hatch within about 10 days. The ammocoetes are immediately washed downstream to slower, deep pools where they bury into the silt bed and remain for up to about five years, living within burrows. They lack a fully developed sucker disc and teeth, their fins are not fully formed, they are blind (although they will react to light) and they are a drab grey-brown that camouflages them against a silty background.

When they have grown to about 10cm, the sucker disc, eyes and fins slowly develop and they attain their sea-going coloration. They head downstream to the sea, usually in May and June, where they feed and grow for up to two years, usually in estuaries and inshore waters. They stop feeding when they return to the river to spawn.

Food and feeding behaviour

Ammocoetes eat algae, bacteria, protozoans and particles of organic detritus that they suck from silt. They emerge at night onto the silt surface and

Most naturalists and anglers never see a lampern. So how will we know if it becomes extinct in a particular river?

hoover at the river bed around their burrow entrance. When they reach saltwater, adult lamperns feed by attaching themselves to fish with their sucker discs and ingesting the blood and digested tissues of their hosts. At the end of a feeding spell their guts can become distended. Lamperns usually feed on herring, mackerel, sprat and, especially important in estuaries, flounders.

Growth and longevity

Lamperns migrating to sea at about five years are only 10–15cm long. They spend one or two years at sea and spawn when they are about 30cm long and weigh 60g. They live for about seven years.

Related species

The Siberian lamprey (Lampetra japonica) is commonly found in rivers draining into the Arctic Ocean from the White Sea eastwards, outside the range of other European lampreys. It is very similar to the lampern in size, shape and appearance, but examination of teeth in the sucker disc will confirm identification. There are lots of large teeth at the front of the sucker disc (lamperns have a few small teeth), and there are three large single or paired teeth at each side of the mouth (lamperns have tiny double or treble teeth).

Conservation status of lampern

This species occurs, often in large numbers, in all rivers within its geographical range provided that the river is clean. It is especially important that the river estuary is clean. Lamperns must travel through estuaries twice in their lives and they often seek a large proportion of their host fish here. In many European rivers damming schemes have exterminated the lampern populations by preventing the upstream migration of returning adults.

Brook Lamprey *Lampetra planeri*

The brook lamprey is one of the smallest European lampreys and it spends its entire life in freshwater, never venturing to sea. It is the only lamprey that does not parasitise other fish.

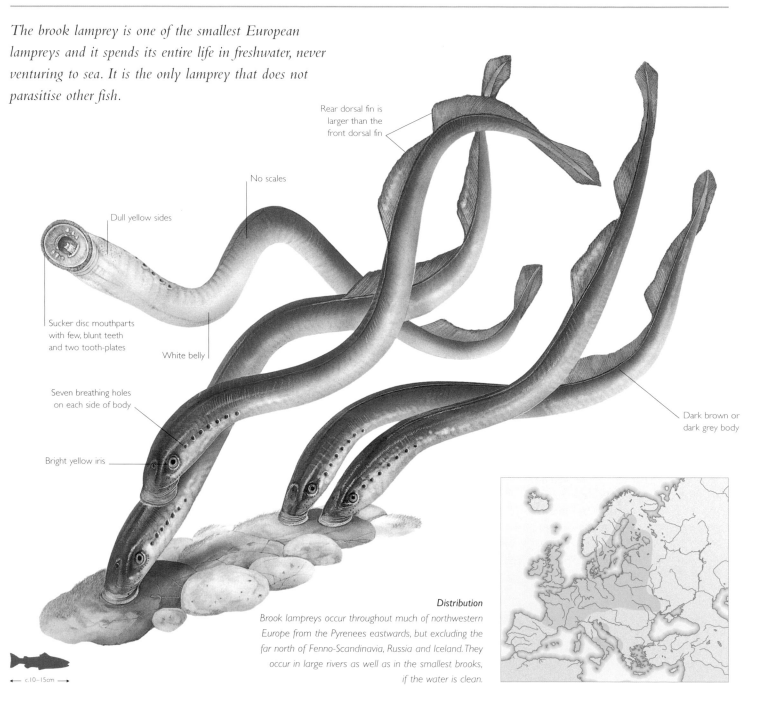

Rear dorsal fin is larger than the front dorsal fin

No scales

Dull yellow sides

Sucker disc mouthparts with few, blunt teeth and two tooth-plates

White belly

Seven breathing holes on each side of body

Bright yellow iris

Dark brown or dark grey body

c.10–15cm

Distribution
Brook lampreys occur throughout much of northwestern Europe from the Pyrenees eastwards, but excluding the far north of Fenno-Scandinavia, Russia and Iceland. They occur in large rivers as well as in the smallest brooks, if the water is clean.

Reaching a maximum length of only 10–15cm, and with its dark coloration, the brook lamprey is often confused for an eel elver (see page 42–43). However, it can be identified by its lack of jaws, paired pectoral fins or gill covers. It also has the characteristic sucker disc mouthparts of lampreys and the line of seven respiratory holes on each side of the body just behind the eye.

The sucker disc has relatively few, fairly blunt, individual teeth and there are two tooth-plates: the front one completely lacks cusps, the rear plate bears six to nine rounded cusps. The two dorsal fins are attached at their bases; the rear and larger dorsal fin tapers and continues into the narrow tail fin. The body is dark brown or dark grey above, shading to dull yellow on the sides and white on the belly. The fins are paler yellow-brown or grey. The iris is bright yellow.

Breeding behaviour and life cycle

Adult brook lampreys remain buried in the silty mud of a river bed until it is breeding time. They then emerge only at night to swim into suitable spawning areas away from the silty juvenile feeding and growing nursery areas: coarse sand or fine gravel through which oxygenated water will flow freely. These spawning areas may be fairly close to nursery areas, such as the streamy tails or necks of deep silty bottomed pools. Sometimes spawning areas may be shallow riffles 400–500m or more downstream of nursery areas.

Temperature triggers these movements: the maturation of eggs and sperm occur early in spring when river temperatures exceed 6–10°C, and mating occurs when the water exceeds 10°C. This is usually during March in much of central and southern Europe, late March and April in the British Isles, Germany, Denmark and Poland, and late April and May farther north in Fenno-Scandinavia and the Baltic States.

Adult brook lampreys gather in spawning knots usually comprising between four and 16 fish (the average is nine to 10), and their initial writhings form a shallow nest in loose sand or gravel. The more fish present in the spawning knot, the bigger the nest. At the sexual climax males attach to females, bodies are entwined, and eggs and sperm are shed simultaneously into the communal nest. The eggs are then covered, but it is not known if only the females do this. All adults die after spawning, usually within two to four days.

The number of eggs produced depends on the how large the female is. Those that are 9cm long produce around 1200 eggs whereas those 16cm long produce around 2400 eggs. The 1mm-diameter, grey-white or pale cream-yellow eggs hatch in four to five days into 3–4mm-long, translucent ammocoete larvae. These larvae emerge from their nest and are washed downstream to deeper, slow pools with silty bottomed nursery areas. Here the ammocoetes burrow and start feeding. Like those of other lampreys, brook lamprey ammocoetes have undeveloped sucker discs and fins, and are blind, although they are light-sensitive and move from light to dark. They gain a drab grey or dull brown coloration.

After two to seven years the fully grown ammocoetes metamorphose into the adult form and coloration, usually in summer or early autumn, but they remain hidden in silt, under boulders or among weeds by day until the spawning season.

Food and feeding behaviour

Ammocoete brook lampreys feed on unicellular algae, protozoans, bacteria and organic detritus. They are quite unselective in their feeding and eat whatever microscopic food particles are available. In captivity, for example, they thrive on a diet of yeast or of phytoplankton strained from lakes. These tiny food particles are sucked into the mouth and stick to strands of mucus that carry the food to the gut. This mucus prevents food from being expelled through the breathing holes. Adult brook lampreys do not feed at all so they never parasitise other fish.

Growth and longevity

The brook lamprey grows slowly to a maximum length of about 10cm in northern, unproductive rivers, and approximately 15cm in southern, more productive rivers. During the winter months between metamorphosis and spawning, when they do not feed, their body length shrinks by about 5 per cent. Maximum life expectancy is six to seven years, when the fish matures, ceases to feed, spawns and then dies.

Predators

Ammocoetes remain hidden from predators within the silt river bed. However adults that have emerged to spawn are often eaten by predatory fish including brown trout and chub, and large water birds such as goosanders. Black-headed and lesser black-backed gulls also take brook lampreys, but usually only dead and dying ones that have spawned. Lampreys were once also highly esteemed as human food and Henry I of England is reputed to have died from eating too many of them in Normandy in 1135.

Related species
Zanandrea's lamprey (Lampetra zanandreai), just 10–15cm long, lives in Italian and Slovenian rivers draining into the northern Adriatic. It is identical to the brook lamprey in general appearance, breeding behaviour and in food and feeding behaviour, but it has been separated from the brook lamprey on the basis that it has only five cusps (not six to nine) on the rear tooth-plate, and double, instead of treble, cusps on the teeth on each side of the mouth. Further research may indicate that it would be wiser to consider this a subspecies, L. planeri zanandreai.

Conservation status of brook lamprey
This is the most abundant European lamprey, although it is easily overlooked. In the River Eden, England, where only single lampreys or a pair were encountered in spring, 129 were collected from a 1.1km stretch following a pollution incidence. Within two years the population had recovered through re-colonisation from a large unaffected population upstream. Unlike sea-going lampreys, brook lampreys are unaffected by estuary pollution and largely unaffected by river damming.

Sturgeon *Acipenser sturio*

Of the seven European species in the Acipenser *genus, six feed and grow in the sea and are now rarely found in freshwater. They are becoming rare and endangered in the wild; stocks for caviar production are farmed.*

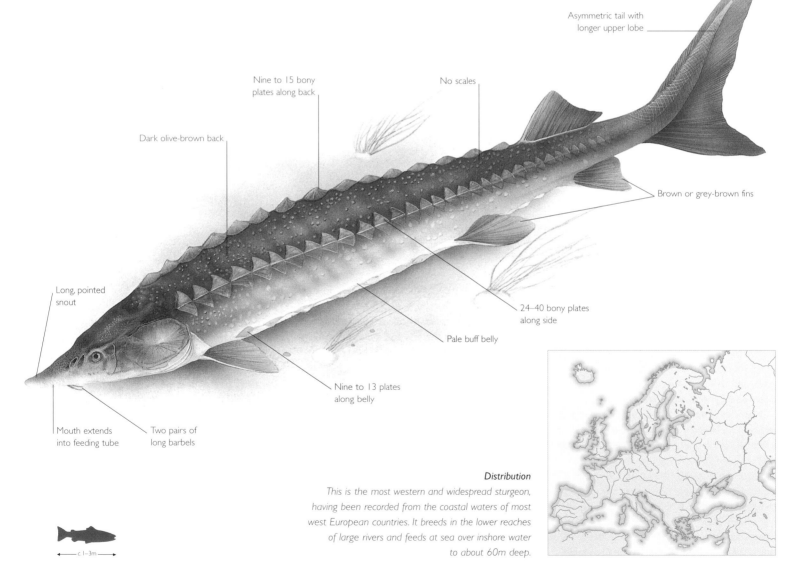

Asymmetric tail with longer upper lobe

Nine to 15 bony plates along back

No scales

Dark olive-brown back

Brown or grey-brown fins

Long, pointed snout

24–40 bony plates along side

Pale buff belly

Nine to 13 plates along belly

Mouth extends into feeding tube

Two pairs of long barbels

c 1–3m

Distribution
This is the most western and widespread sturgeon, having been recorded from the coastal waters of most west European countries. It breeds in the lower reaches of large rivers and feeds at sea over inshore water to about 60m deep.

The sturgeon is easily identified by its elongated shape, long, pointed snout and a mouth that extends into a feeding tube. It also has an asymmetric tail with a longer upper lobe and five rows of conspicuous bony plates running the length of the body on the back, sides and belly. There are nine to 15 plates in the row running along the back, 24 to 40 plates in the side rows and nine to 13 in the belly rows. There are two pairs of long, smooth barbels between the tip of the snout and the mouth. Scales are lacking, and the skin is soft and smooth between the bony plates. The back is dark olive-brown or, in old specimens, almost black, and the belly is pale buff. The fins are brown or grey-brown.

Breeding behaviour and life cycle
Adult sturgeon enter the lower reaches of rivers from the sea in late winter, and spawn in late March to June in fast turbulent water at least 2m deep over clean gravel. The female sheds up to 250,000 2–2.5mm-diameter, brown eggs, which are fertilised by the male. The fertilised eggs are much denser than water and sticky so they sink into the gravel and adhere to stones. The 10mm larvae hatch after about six days at water temperatures of 14–16°C or three to four days at 19–20°C. The young remain in the lower reaches of the river for two or three years before eventually moving into

The roe from a female sturgeon is a gourmet's delight, caviar. Although wild sturgeon stocks are endangered, the profits from caviar ensure the survival of this fish.

the estuary and out to sea. Males spend at least four, and females at least five, years feeding at sea before they mature and make their first spawning run. After spawning, adult sturgeon head back to sea and return to spawn again the following year.

Food and feeding behaviour
Sturgeon fry feed on bottom invertebrates, including midge and caddis larvae, freshwater shrimps and snails in the river. Adults that have returned to the river to spawn do not feed, but at sea they feed on or close to the sea bed to about 60m deep. Here they eat small fish, such as sand-eels, gobies and other fish fry, and invertebrates including bivalved molluscs, snails, polychaete worms and shrimps.

Growth and longevity
One-year-old sturgeon are 10–12cm, and 20cm at two years old. Mature males are 1–1.5m at four to six years old; females grow to 1.2–1.8m from five to nine years old. Sturgeon can grow very large, up to 3m, exceptionally 3.5m, long. Reported maximum weights are over 200kg. Sturgeon have been reported living for more than 100 years.

Related species
The following sturgeon are native of the Black, Caspian and Adriatic Seas and the rivers draining into them. They are now very rare in the wild, although some of them are farmed for their caviar:

- Adriatic sturgeon (Acipenser naccarii), which has 32–42 plates in its side rows.
- Russian sturgeon (Acipenser guldenstaedti), which has 25–50 plates in its side rows.
- Ship sturgeon (Acipenser nudiventris), which has at least 60 sharply pointed plates in its side rows.
- Stellate sturgeon (Acipenser stellatus), which has 30–40 plates in its side rows.
- Beluga (Huso huso), which has 40–60 plates in its side rows.

The beluga is the greatest of all sturgeons and reaches 5m and weights in excess of 1 tonne. It is a very heavily built fish with a short, wide snout, a wide mouth and long barbels. The population has declined in the last 50 years, and it is now almost certainly extinct in the Adriatic. Its survival today depends largely on the fact that it is farmed for caviar in the Black Sea. When all the beluga are born in hatcheries, the species will no longer be truly wild. The future of most sturgeon species is in these hatcheries – if this majestic fish didn't produce caviar, it would become extinct.

Another species has been introduced to eastern Europe from Asia, namely the Siberian sturgeon (Acipenser baeri).

Conservation status of sturgeon
Many centuries ago this fish probably spawned in most major rivers, such as the Rhine, Thames, Severn and Shannon, but over-fishing, pollution and damming have greatly reduced its breeding range. Now it spawns regularly only in the Danube, Gironde and Rioni rivers, and must be considered one of the most endangered freshwater fish in Europe.

Sterlet *Acipenser rutheneus*

The sterlet is a distinctive sturgeon, which is easy to identify. It spends its entire life in freshwater and tends to be a much smaller species than the six other anadromous sturgeons.

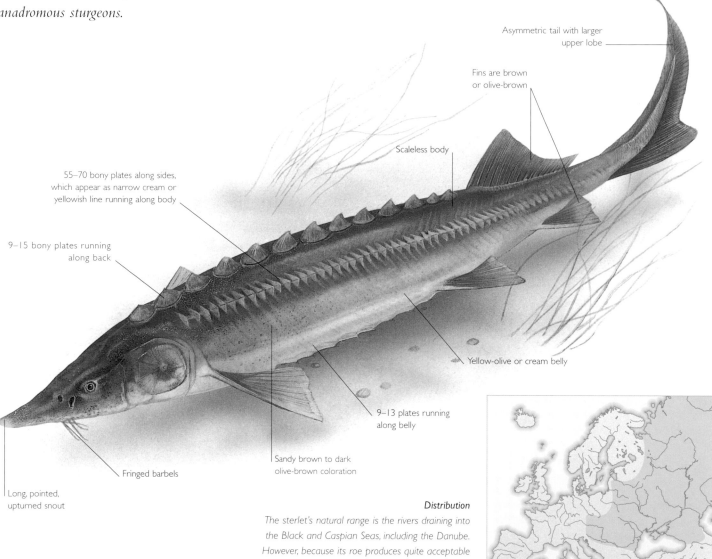

Asymmetric tail with larger upper lobe

Fins are brown or olive-brown

Scaleless body

55–70 bony plates along sides, which appear as narrow cream or yellowish line running along body

9–15 bony plates running along back

Yellow-olive or cream belly

9–13 plates running along belly

Sandy brown to dark olive-brown coloration

Fringed barbels

Long, pointed, upturned snout

c.80cm

Distribution

The sterlet's natural range is the rivers draining into the Black and Caspian Seas, including the Danube. However, because its roe produces quite acceptable caviar and its flesh is meat of good quality, it has been brought into captivity by the Russians and used to stock other rivers and lakes.

The sterlet is easy to identify as a sturgeon by its elongated, streamlined body, long pointed snout and asymmetric tail with the upper lobe much larger than the lower. The body is scaleless, the skin smooth and soft, and there are five rows of bony plates running down the body, one along the back, two along the belly and one along each side. Besides its much smaller size, the sterlet is readily separated from other sturgeons because of its fringed barbels, which are smooth and unfringed in anadromous sturgeons, upturned snout, which is straight in others, and the 55 to 70 tiny plates in the side rows of its body.

The background body colour varies from a sandy brown to a dark olive-brown, with a yellow-olive or cream belly; the side rows of plates are much lighter in colour and can look like a narrow cream or yellowish line running along the body. The fins are brown or olive-brown.

Breeding behaviour and life cycle

At the end of winter, as the water warms, adult sterlets move upstream to their spawning areas, shallow, turbulent riffles flowing over fine, clean gravel in clean river headwaters. Males arrive before females and mating occurs in May–June. No nest is made; instead a pair lies side by side close to the gravel with their bodies touching. The female sheds her eggs, the male releases his sperm-carrying milt and the fertilised eggs fall to the gravel where they stick to the stones. After spawning the adults return downstream to their feeding areas.

Each female produces roughly 10,000 2.7 × 2.2mm-diameter, brown, ovoid eggs per kilogram of her body weight. The 10mm larvae hatch after about four days at water temperatures of 12–15°C and soon begin to feed on microscopic organisms, moving into sheltered shallows where fish predators are less likely to occur. In their first autumn they begin to spread downstream towards the deep-water adult feeding areas.

Food and feeding behaviour

Both immature and adult sterlets predominantly feed on river-bed invertebrates, sucking them from the bottom in a hoover-like fashion with

Notice how the sterlet, the only sturgeon that does not go to sea, uses its fringed barbels to feel along the river bed to search for food.

their long tubular mouths. Stomach analyses suggest that they devour a representative sample of the large invertebrates occurring in a river: mayfly nymphs and the larvae of chironomid midges and caddisflies often feature, as well as aquatic snails, worms and, where they are abundant, freshwater shrimps. They are also reputed to take eggs of other fish species, notably those of cyprinids. Those sterlets that move downstream as far as brackish water feed on estuarine prawns and shrimps, small crabs, tiny snails and worms.

Sterlets are summer feeders – they begin to feed after spawning is over (non-breeding immature sterlets start in April or May) in the clean, lower reaches of rivers, including, in some rivers, brackish estuaries, and larger lakes. They virtually stop feeding with the arrival of low water temperatures in the winter (late October or November), although they will take the occasional piece of food.

Growth and longevity

At the end of the first year young sterlets are 8–10cm. Thereafter growth is steady until the fish attain sexual maturity, which in males is at three to four years and 30–35cm long, and in females four to five years and 35–40cm. Most sterlets grow to a maximum length of about 80cm and weights of

about 2.5–2.7kg at 12 to15 years of age. Exceptional records are of a fish that was 1.22m long and weighed 15.8kg. It was aged at over 20 years old.

Predators

Small, immature sterlets are a food source for fish-eating fish such as pike, asp and zander, and birds including cormorants and grey herons. Adult sturgeons are a popular angler's quarry in easten Europe and a prized table fish.

Twaite Shad *Alosa fallax*

The twaite shad is a member of the herring family that spends most of its life at sea, returning to freshwater only to spawn. Populations have declined due to pollution and river damming.

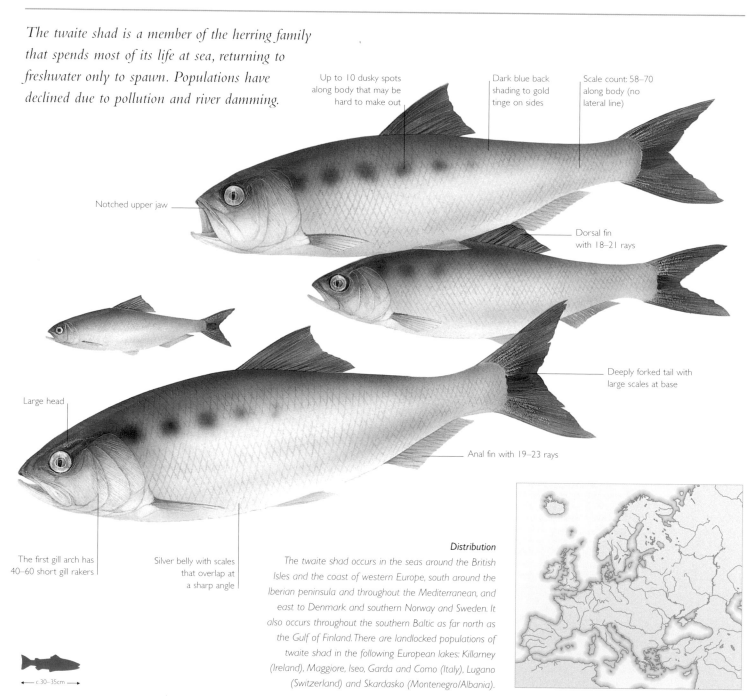

Up to 10 dusky spots along body that may be hard to make out

Dark blue back shading to gold tinge on sides

Scale count: 58–70 along body (no lateral line)

Notched upper jaw

Dorsal fin with 18–21 rays

Deeply forked tail with large scales at base

Large head

Anal fin with 19–23 rays

The first gill arch has 40–60 short gill rakers

Silver belly with scales that overlap at a sharp angle

← c.30–35cm →

Distribution
The twaite shad occurs in the seas around the British Isles and the coast of western Europe, south around the Iberian peninsula and throughout the Mediterranean, and east to Denmark and southern Norway and Sweden. It also occurs throughout the southern Baltic as far north as the Gulf of Finland. There are landlocked populations of twaite shad in the following European lakes: Killarney (Ireland), Maggiore, Iseo, Garda and Como (Italy), Lugano (Switzerland) and Skardasko (Montenegro/Albania).

All shads are identified by their deep, keeled, silvery body that is flattened side-to-side; when examined from the side, the belly appears to be toothed because of the way the scales overlap at a sharp angle. The tiny scales are easily detached when the fish is handled; the deeply forked tail has large leaf-like scales at its base and lines of tiny scales radiating across it. There is no lateral line. The head is large. The upper jaw is notched, and the tip of the lower jaw fits into this notch when the mouth is closed. The gill cover has a network of fine furrows radiating across it. The eyes have thin, transparent fatty membranes covering the front and rear portions.

In twaite shads the back is dark blue, shading to a gold tinge on the sides and silver below. There are usually six to 10 dusky spots running along the sides of the body from just behind the gill cover to level with the dorsal fin. Sometimes these are very indistinct, sometimes absent and sometimes only one or two may be visible.

Breeding behaviour and life cycle

The twaite shads return from the sea to rivers to spawn between late April and early June and in exceptional cases as late as July. The biggest movements of adult shads from the sea occur on spring tides that help lift the shoals of fish quickly from the estuary and into their freshwater spawning reaches. Spawning occurs in June, usually under cover of darkness in streamy, well-oxygenated pool necks. Each female produces over 100,000 tiny (1.5mm-diameter) eggs, which are fertilised by the males. Large females can produce up to 200,000 eggs. After fertilisation the eggs swell to about 4mm in diameter by absorbing water and are washed downstream to drift with the tide over estuarine sand and silt.

The 8–10mm-long larvae hatch after a minimum of two to three days, if the water temperature is 21°C or more, or a maximum of eight to 10 days if the water is 12–14°C. They remain in the lower river reaches or estuary feeding as fry until the autumn when they head for the open sea. Adult shads return to sea immediately after they have spawned. Landlocked lake forms of twaite shad spawn in spring over

gravel in riffles in inflowing streams, and the developing eggs drift slowly downstream towards the lake. Adult shads take little, if any, food during their spawning run – the stomachs of seven were found to be empty, and that of an eighth was found to contain a tiny amount of unidentifiable digested pulp.

Food and feeding behaviour

In the lower reaches of the river and estuary the twaite shad fry feed initially on food items that are often no more than about 1mm in length, including tiny planktonic crustaceans, larval worms and molluscs.

At sea this species is a shoaling fish, feeding mainly in inshore waters and usually in mid- or surface depths, although it has been reported feeding as deep as 100m. The foods are again primarily planktonic crustaceans or larger crustaceans, such as shrimps and mysid prawns, which themselves are feeding on plankton.

When feeding on plankton the twaite shad is a filter-feeder – water containing oxygen and food particles flows in the fish's mouth as it swims. Oxygen is removed by the gill filaments, the plankton is filtered out by the gill rakers and the water is expelled via the gill cover. Lake forms of twaite shad feed by filtering planktonic crustaceans, such as *Daphnia* and *Mysis*, and insect larvae including the planktonic phantom-fly larvae *Chaoborus* from the epilimnion, and midge pupae rising to hatch at the water surface. Lake forms virtually stop feeding during the winter months, when the populations of planktonic organisms are very low.

Growth and longevity

Fry feeding in the estuary grow to approximately 5cm long after six months. At one year of age they reach 10–15cm; 20–25cm at two years; 25–30cm at three years, when most males mature; and 30–35cm at five years, when most females mature. Their maximum length is about 50–55cm and maximum weight is about 2kg, with exceptional records as heavy as 3.5kg. Twaite shad normally live for 15 to 20 years but have been know to reach 25 years of age on rare occasions.

Predators

At sea, fry feature in the diets of terns and gulls, and also in the diets of divers, grebes and fish-eating sea ducks, including the red-breasted merganser, during the winter months. Larger twaite shads are also eaten by cormorants.

In the river, twaite shads have very few predators, although a large pike or a comorant that has flown upstream might devour one. Despite the publication of early recipes featuring twaite shads, they tend to be too bony a fish to be very popular amongst humans.

Related species
The Black Sea sprat (Clupeonella cultriventris) is a very small (up to 15cm), very slender fish with a large, upturned mouth and slightly protruding lower jaw. When viewed from the side, the scales on the belly represent a marked, toothed appearance on the lower profile of the fish. It has a blue- or green-grey back, silver sides and a white belly. It feeds by filtering planktonic invertebrates from the Black Sea, often at depths of up to 70m. Although primarily a marine fish, the Black Sea sprat may be found in the lower reaches of rivers draining into the Black Sea, where they spawn. They make two spawning runs, one in spring and one in autumn.

Conservation status of twaite shad
Once common and widespread, this fish is now extinct or almost extinct in many rivers primarily because of pollution in estuaries and lower freshwater reaches. Runs have been exterminated in some rivers because of dam construction, which has prevented shads from passing upstream to their spawning areas. Even though there are still several rivers with healthy runs of fish, this species ought to be considered endangered and special efforts made, such as removing pollution threats and constructing easy-access fish passes in dams, to protect those runs that still exist.

Pike *Esox lucius*

The pike is the best-known European predatory fish with a reputation for evil malevolence. It is big and powerful with large, cold eyes and immense jaws bristling with huge, sharp fangs.

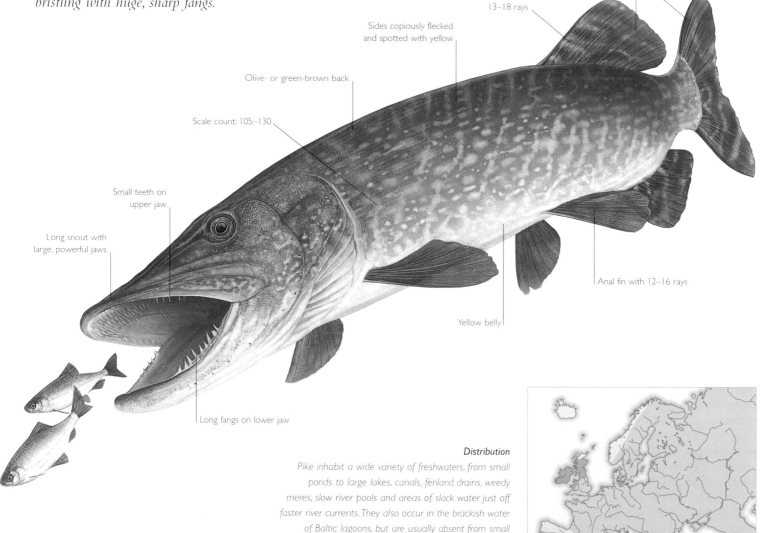

Dorsal, anal and tail fins are close together and produce fast acceleration

Dorsal fin with 13–18 rays

Sides copiously flecked and spotted with yellow

Olive- or green-brown back

Scale count: 105–130

Small teeth on upper jaw

Long snout with large, powerful jaws

Long fangs on lower jaw

Anal fin with 12–16 rays

Yellow belly

← c.75cm–1m →

Distribution

Pike inhabit a wide variety of freshwaters, from small ponds to large lakes, canals, fenland drains, weedy meres, slow river pools and areas of slack water just off faster river currents. They also occur in the brackish water of Baltic lagoons, but are usually absent from small mountain lakes. Pike are widespread through most of Europe except for parts of the far north, Iberia and the far south. They have been introduced to several areas where they do not occur naturally.

Pike are identified by their streamlined, elongated body with long snout and large, powerful jaws. The dorsal and anal fins are opposite each other and close to the tail fin so all three act together to produce rapid acceleration over short distances.

Coloration varies, but is generally olive- or green-brown, shading to yellow on the belly; in weedy waters coloration tends to be more green, in brackish water it is more yellow or pale olive, and in peat-stained waters it is browner. Once the pattern of yellow markings has developed on its sides, it remains fairly constant throughout a pike's life and, like finger prints, can be used to identify individuals that have been caught on several occasions over a number of years. The large dorsal, tail and anal fins are olive-brown flecked yellow; the pectorals and pelvics are yellow-brown.

Breeding behaviour and life cycle

Pike spawn in spring, from the end of March in the south of its range to late June in arctic waters. The adults move from deeper water, sometimes several weeks before spawning time, into the spawning areas, which are usually weedy and often no more than 25cm deep.

Males often arrive before the females. When a female is ready to shed her eggs she is joined by several males, one of which lies alongside her 'eye-to-eye'. She releases a batch of eggs and the male fertilises them. It is thought that male pike have evolved to be much shorter than females to aid fertilisation: when lying eye-to-eye the sperm passes back through the eggs being shed by the female. If both males' and females' vents were side-by-side, much of the sperm would be liberated behind the eggs, reducing the chance of fertilisation. Should the first male be unable to produce sufficient sperm to fertilise all the eggs produced by a big female, another male will take his place when he is 'spent'.

The yellow-brown, 2.5mm-diameter eggs are laid as a brown, sticky mass on vegetation. Each female produces approximately 50,000 per kilogram of her body weight. It is not unusual, in a large lake, to find one patch of water weed covered with spawn while other apparently similar weedbeds have none.

Pike sometimes swim into water meadows or an area of flooded fields to spawn. However, should the spate fall or the water meadows dry up before the eggs have hatched, an entire year's egg production may be lost. For this reason a river or lake pike population may have one or more 'year classes' completely missing.

The eggs hatch within 10–15 days or up to 25 days in cold northern waters. A larval pike digests the remains of its yolk sac then, at about 12mm long, the mouth develops and the fry swims off in search of planktonic food. It begins to eat tiny fish when it is 5cm long.

Food and feeding behaviour

Pike will devour any fish smaller than themselves. Preferred prey size appears to be 10–25 per cent of an individual's body weight and records of pike taking a prey up to 50 per cent of their own weight are not rare. Pike will also eat ducklings, young moorhens, coot and grebes, gulls, frogs, toads and newts, and smaller aquatic mammals such as water voles, brown rats and water shrews. On one lake, a major winter food is black-headed gulls, which are caught at dusk and night as they are roosting on the water. There are reports of small dogs, swimming to retrieve sticks, being seized by mammoth pike.

Magnificent pike: the aquatic tiger!

Growth and longevity

In a study of four lakes, the average size in males was 26cm at one year and 76cm at seven years. Females were 26cm at one year and 99cm at seven years.

Male pike mature at two to three years old, females at three to five. Few males live for more than 10 years and exceed weights of 5kg, whereas females may continue growing through a life span of over 25 years. Many old female pike reach 15kg and there are records of a few that have passed the 30kg barrier.

Predators

Small pike are a major source of food for ospreys in Fenno-Scandinavia and Scotland. Large pike are the main predators of small pike in many waters.

Conservation status of pike
Pike stocks are thriving throughout most of their range. This is at least partly because anglers think highly of them and carefully protect pike populations, reintroducing them to waters where the species has been lost.

European Mudminnow *Umbra krameri*

This tiny little fish lives in oxygen-lacking swamps, marshes, ponds and river backwaters. It is rarely seen, simply because few naturalists research such places and it is never caught by anglers.

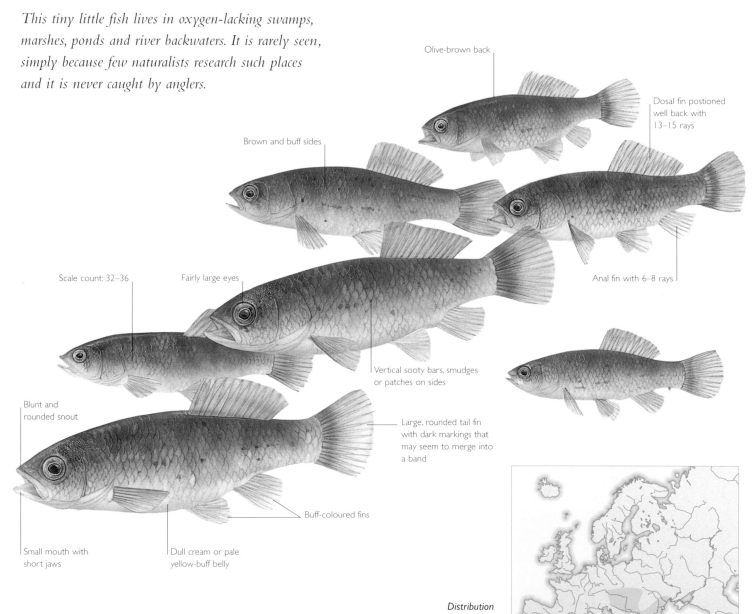

Olive-brown back

Dosal fin postioned well back with 13–15 rays

Brown and buff sides

Anal fin with 6–8 rays

Scale count: 32–36

Fairly large eyes

Vertical sooty bars, smudges or patches on sides

Blunt and rounded snout

Large, rounded tail fin with dark markings that may seem to merge into a band

Buff-coloured fins

Small mouth with short jaws

Dull cream or pale yellow-buff belly

c.6–8cm

Distribution

The European mudminnow lives in very weedy swamps, ponds, sluggish streams and shallow, overgrown margins in the Danube basin. These waters are often so low in oxygen that their only fish inhabitant is the mudminnow.

The mudminnow is a small, stockily built fish with a dorsal fin, which has a base about twice the length of the anal fin base, positioned well back on the body. Both the pelvic and anal fins are opposite the dorsal fin, and the tail fin is large and rounded. The head is fairly large, the snout blunt and rounded, the mouth is small with short jaws and the eyes are fairly large. Scales extend over the entire body and head.

Overall coloration is a camouflaged mix of brown and buff. The back is olive-brown, the sides a lighter buff or yellow-brown, with indistinct vertical sooty bars, smudges or patches, and the belly is dull cream or pale yellow-buff. All the fins are buff, the tail fin is often darker, and there may sometimes be slightly darker brown markings on the tail fin and dorsal fin. The markings on the tail fin might appear to merge into a band close to the fin base.

Breeding behaviour and life cycle

Spawning occurs during the months of March or April (and occasionally as early as February or as late as May) in shallow, weedy water. The female chooses a hollow on the bottom of the water among weeds and lays a small number (usually up to approximately 140, but occasionally more than 200 in large specimens) of 1.5mm brown eggs that stick to weeds or to the bottom. The male mudminnow fertilises them and departs while the female remains to guard the eggs, removing any dead ones that may infect the living and preventing silt and dead, decaying vegetation from choking them, until they hatch approximately five days later. The 7–8mm larvae attach to nearby weeds until their yolk sacs are exhausted; they then disperse and feed on tiny crustaceans, especially ostracods and copepods.

Food and feeding behaviour

Mudminnows are bottom-feeders, taking whatever invertebrates are available. In most mudminnow habitats this includes many species that can tolerate low oxygen levels, including bloodworm, water hog-lice and aquatic worms. In areas that have higher oxygen levels, mudminnows eat small caddis larvae, pond snails, pea-mussels, freshwater shrimps and both lesser and greater waterboatmen, *Corixa* and *Notonecta*. Stomach analyses have also revealed that they feed on the larvae and adults of aquatic beetles, and dragonfly and damselfly nymphs.

Growth and longevity

Females are always larger than males of the same age. After one year males average about 4cm long, after two years they measure approximately 5.5cm and 6.5cm after three years. Females average about 4.5cm long after one year, after two years they are about 7cm and after three years 8.5cm. Females live for about five years (six years in captivity) when they may grow to 10cm (exceptionally 12cm) long.

Predators

The European mudminnow lives in waters that often contain few other fish species: crucian carp and pond loach are most likely to be its neighbours. These sometimes eat the mudminnow's eggs or larvae. So too might large dragonfly nymphs and the carnivorous larvae of the great diving beetle *Dytiscus*. In reed-fringed lakes, for instance, in the Neusiedler See on the Austrian–Hungarian border, small immature mudminnows are food for kingfishers, egrets and little bitterns; adults mudminnows are eaten by grey and purple herons and bitterns.

Habitat survival

The European mudminnow lives in very weedy swamps, ponds, sluggish streams and shallow, overgrown margins. These waters are often so low in oxygen levels that their only fish inhabitant is the mudminnow. How these tiny fish are able to survive in such a hostile environment is not yet fully understood because they do not appear to swim to the surface to gulp gaseous oxygen as might be expected. One hypothesis is that their haemoglobin, the oxygen-carrying red pigment in the blood, is capable of being fully saturated with oxygen even when there are only extremely low concentrations of oxygen in the water. In contrast, the haemoglobin of other fish species requires much higher levels of oxygen in the water in order to become as saturated. So mudminnows are able to obtain enough oxygen to enable them to survive in water where other species such as trout would immediately die because of a lack of oxygen.

In winter, when the previous summer's vegetation has died back and is slowly decomposing, mudminnows may be locked in water under ice almost completely lacking in oxygen. Their survival then is due in part at least to their metabolic rate and minimal oxygen needs – so minimal that it is very difficult to detect any signs of life in the little fish.

Related species
The American mudminnow, sometimes known as the Eastern mudminnow (Umbra pygmaea), has a very similar structure and coloration to the European mudminnow, but it has a distinguishing, distinct dark patch at the base of its tail and alternating bands of olive-brown and green-olive running down the length of its body. It reaches a maximum length of about 10cm. Its feeding habits and breeding behaviour are similar to those of the European mudminnow. Originally introduced from North America as an aquarium fish, this species has been released into a few, usually weedy, shallow pools in northern Germany, Holland and France. Like the European mudminnow, it is able to survive in water that is almost completely lacking in oxygen.

Conservation status of European mudminnow
This fascinating little fish is declining due to drainage of swamps and shallow meres and the neatening and canalisation of river banks. It should be considered a threatened species in the wild. The European mudminnow is very easy to keep in aquaria and garden pools, and these might be useful ways of ensuring the species' survival should wild stocks be exterminated. These captive fish could then be used to restock suitable wetland nature reserves.

Atlantic Salmon *Salmo salar*

One of the most spectacular European fish with a most remarkable life cycle, the salmon is born in the river, feeds far out at sea and returns to freshwater to spawn.

Male

Female

9–13, usually 11, scales between adipose fin and lateral line

Red-brown coloration is found in male only

'Wrist' at base of tail

Steel-grey back and silvery sides typical in female

Dorsal fin with 9–12 rays

Scale count: 109–130

Black spots on gill covers

Forked tail fin

Anal fin with 8–11 rays

Elongated snout and hooked lower jaw are typical in male

Slender gill rakers on first gill arch

Jaw extends no farther back than rear of the eye

← c.50cm–1m →

Distribution

The salmon occurs in all European rivers from northern Spain northwards where the water is pollution-free and there are no high dams, waterfalls or weirs blocking the river. Salmon also pass through lakes as they move to spawning streams. There are some landlocked salmon populations: Lake Ladoga (Russia), Vanern (Sweden) and several lakes on the River Otra (Norway).

Adult salmon are easily identified by their steel-grey back and silvery sides merging to white on the belly. There are usually a few black spots on the dorsal surface and gill covers. Like all members of the family, salmon have a small, fleshy adipose fin. After the fish have been in freshwater for some time the silver sheen begins to fade and males develop a rich tartan of reds and browns. This coloration appears as an overtone to a dominantly grey background in hen salmon. The female's head remains short, but the cock's jaw and snout elongate and the lower jaw develops a long, hooked structure called a 'kype'.

Breeding behaviour and life cycle

Salmon spawn in fast-flowing rivers from October to January. The female cuts a 15cm-deep nest or 'redd' in coarse gravel and sheds a batch of eggs, which is then fertilised by the male's milt. The eggs are then covered with gravel. Each female produces about 1500 eggs per kilogram of her body weight. Sexually mature male parr (or 'precocious parr') often attend spawning salmon and also shed milt, increasing chances of fertilisation.

After spawning almost all cock fish die. A higher proportion of hens (usually about 10 per cent) survive as kelts and spawn for a second time. It is rare, however, for a salmon to spawn three times. Some kelts return to sea immediately after spawning, others spend several more weeks in the river before returning to sea. Kelts take no food until they reach the sea.

The 6mm-diameter orange eggs hatch after seven to 22 weeks (normally about 12 weeks) into alevins, 2cm-long larvae, which still have prominent yolk sacs that provide food. Alevins remain in the gravel redd and become fry once their yolk sacs have been absorbed. Initially fry eat tiny particles of organic matter from water taken into the mouth during respiration, but as they grow they swim up through the gravel and begin to hunt food. As the fry grow larger they develop a camouflaged coloration that includes a series of oval, dark grey markings along the sides. These are parr-marks, and the young fish, now about 7cm long, are known as parr. Salmon parr can often be confused for trout parr (see pages 50–51).

When, in spring, salmon parr reach a threshold length of 13cm and develop the physiology that will enable them to cope with saltwater life, they become silver smolts and head off to sea. Most smolts from European rivers head to feeding areas around the Faeroe Islands, the Norwegian Sea or off the west coast of Greenland where they mix with Atlantic salmon smolts from eastern North America. Some of these fish, referred to as grilse, return to their native rivers after just one winter at sea. Others remain feeding at sea for two or three years before they return.

The vast majority of salmon return, not only to their natal rivers, but to the tributary of their birth. At sea they migrate close to the water surface, and use the sun, moon and stars, the earth's magnetic field and prevailing sea currents as navigational aids. The final movement into their home estuary is based on the 'smell' or 'taste' of the river.

Food and feeding behaviour

Salmon parr feed on a wide range of invertebrates. At sea the growing salmon feed on fish, including capelin, sand-eels, herring, sprats and small cod. They also eat squid and a variety of crustaceans including krill. Adult salmon rarely take items of food on their return migration or in freshwater.

The hooked lower jaw, or kype, on this salmon indicates that it is a male.

Growth and longevity

Smolts average 13cm in length. On their return to freshwater, salmon usually weigh 1.5–5kg after approximately one year at sea (grilse); 4–14kg after approximately two years at sea; and over 10.5kg after about three years at sea.

Predators

Parr and smolts are a major source of food for birds, such as goosanders and cormorants, and adult salmon are prey for grey seals. In some areas, this has resulted in a conflict between naturalists and anglers.

Conservation status of Atlantic salmon
The salmon is currently not endangered, but its population is very low. This is primarily because higher than normal Atlantic Sea temperatures are greatly increasing mortality on the marine feeding grounds. At the same time, while gross pollution is being reduced in many regions, poor physical river conditions (see pages 16–19) are preventing many rivers from producing their optimal number of smolts.

Brown Trout *Salmo trutta*

The brown trout is one of the most widespread European fish and one of the most popular among anglers and gourmets. It is extremely variable in size, coloration and behaviour.

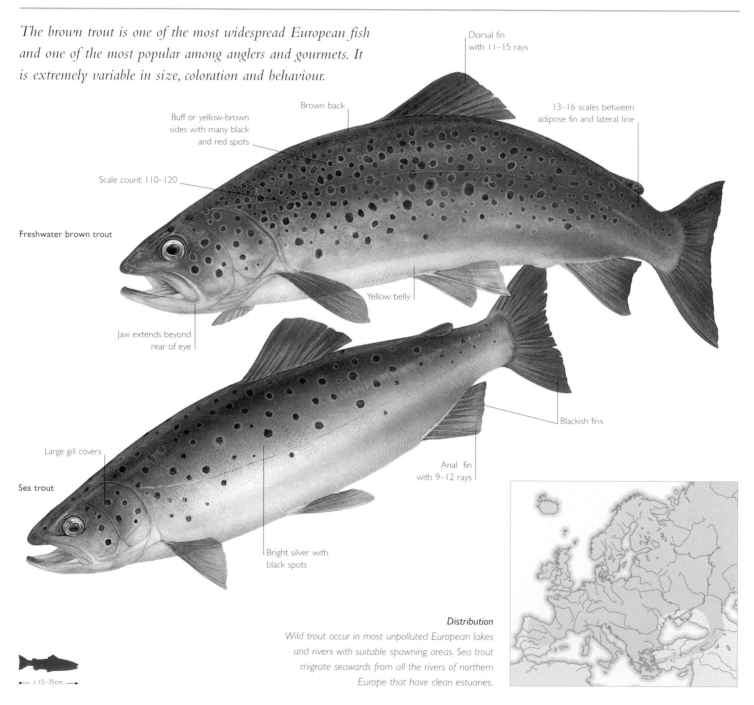

Dorsal fin with 11–15 rays

Brown back

13–16 scales between adipose fin and lateral line

Buff or yellow-brown sides with many black and red spots

Scale count: 110–120

Freshwater brown trout

Yellow belly

Jaw extends beyond rear of eye

Blackish fins

Large gill covers

Anal fin with 9–12 rays

Sea trout

Bright silver with black spots

c.15–35cm

Distribution
Wild trout occur in most unpolluted European lakes and rivers with suitable spawning areas. Sea trout migrate seawards from all the rivers of northern Europe that have clean estuaries.

All forms of *Salmo trutta* can be identified by a slightly flattened, streamlined body that has a maximum depth in front of the dorsal fin. There is no spotting on the tail fin and there is a deep caudal peduncle or 'wrist' at the base of the tail.

The most widespread form is the brown trout, which is resident in freshwater. Coloration is highly variable and some brown trout may appear silvery, whereas others are a very drab black-brown. By contrast sea trout, *Salmo trutta* that migrate to sea, return to the river with a black-spotted, bright silver coloration, which can make them difficult to identify from small salmon (see pages 48-49). Many other forms have been described including the big, fish-eating 'ferox' trout from deep, oligotrophic lakes, the gaudy 'gillaroo' of Irish lake margins, the steel-grey, black-finned 'sonaghen' uniquely found in Lough Melvin, the drab slob trout that feeds in estuaries, and the large-spotted trout, often classified as *S. trutta macrostigmata* from southern Greece, Sicily, Corsica and Sardinia and *S. trutta dentax* from the eastern Adriatic rivers.

Breeding behaviour and life cycle

Adult trout pair and spawn in small, shallow streams between late September and December (occasionally as late as February). The orange, 5mm-diameter eggs are laid in a redd cut by the female in pea-sized gravel. They are immediately fertilised by the male and then covered with gravel by the female. Each female produces about 1000 to 1500 eggs per kilogram of her body weight.

The eggs hatch into alevins after six to nine weeks and feed on their yolk sacs for a further four to six weeks. Then they emerge from the redd as fry to hunt for food. As fry grow they develop a camouflaged coloration, including dusky markings along the sides, and are known as parr. After one to three years, the freshwater fish assume adult coloration and move to appropriate feeding areas. Most brown trout undergo some migrations: lake forms head to the lake; river trout usually move downstream into deeper water; slob trout move down to the estuary; and those parr that give rise to sea trout lose their drab river coloration, become silver smolts and head to sea. Unlike salmon, sea trout tend to remain close to the shore, feeding in estuaries, fjords and bays.

Food and feeding behaviour

Smaller trout, including lake and river forms, feed predominantly on invertebrates, but they will also take wind-blown land insects from the surface. All trout will also take lesser fish, including minnows, and fry. However, larger lake forms, such as ferox, eat lesser fish, usually arctic char or whitefish. In estuaries and at sea, slob trout and sea trout eat shrimps, prawns, crabs and fish.

Growth and longevity

In acid, oligotrophic lakes brown trout average 10–15cm after three years, whereas in mesotrophic lakes and chalkstreams, trout measure 30cm or more. Most ordinary brown trout, whether lake or river, mature at two to three years; few live beyond five to six years. By contrast, ferox are long-lived trout. A ferox from a Norwegian lake weighed 16.4kg and was 18 years old. Sea trout smolts average about 15cm when they go to sea and many return to the river after only a few months at 25–30cm long, weighing about 400g.

Predators

Fry are often eaten by kingfishers, parr by perch, chub, larger trout and goosanders, and adult trout by cormorants and otters.

Conservation status of brown trout

In many rivers and some lakes the effects of pollution and over-fishing have caused a collapse of brown trout stocks. Artificial restocking with hatchery-bred trout has often been seen as a remedy, but this threatens the wild trout strain by replacing it with a fish-farm stock that has a high mortality rate and low reproductive success. In contrast, many rivers and lakes have lost their stocks of sea trout through river damming and the effects of salmon farming, especially off western Ireland and western and northern Scotland. Sea trout smolts are killed by the high densities of sea lice living in and around the offshore salmon farms. Thousands of sea trout once fed around the Shetland Islands; today, consequent to intensive salmon farming, there are none.

Powan *Coregonus lavaretus*

The classification of all the Coregonus *whitefish is complex and few scientists agree on what are the true species. The powan is called 'schelly' in the English Lake District and 'gwyniad' in its only Welsh lake, Llyn Tegid.*

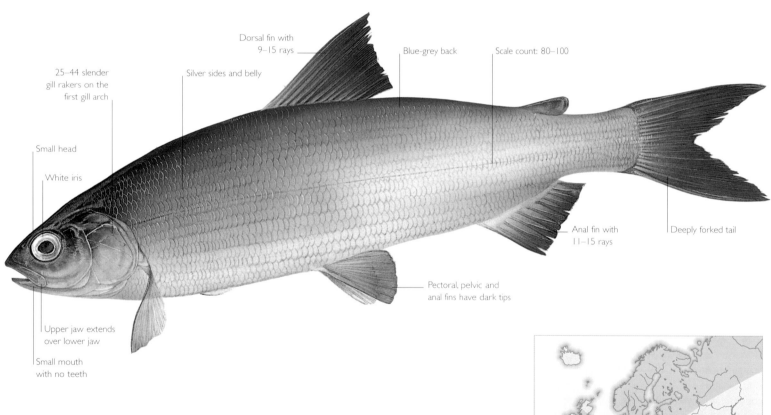

Dorsal fin with 9–15 rays

Blue-grey back

Scale count: 80–100

25–44 slender gill rakers on the first gill arch

Silver sides and belly

Small head

White iris

Small mouth with no teeth

Upper jaw extends over lower jaw

Pectoral, pelvic and anal fins have dark tips

Anal fin with 11–15 rays

Deeply forked tail

c.25cm

Distribution

There are many isolated lake populations throughout the Alps, British Isles (but not Ireland), Fenno-Scandinavia, the Baltic States and Russia. River populations exist in Arctic Russia. The migratory form, houting, occurs in good numbers in the Baltic and rivers draining into that sea, but it has become very rare, maybe extinct, in the North Sea basin.

The powan is typically salmonid in appearance with a slender, streamlined build. The head is small, the fairly small mouth lacks teeth and is on the underside of the snout. The upper jaw is usually longer than the lower jaw. Mouth structure is a major feature used to separate the three European whitefish species, but it is highly variable. In some populations the upper jaw extension is virtually non-existent, whereas the houting (the migratory form) has a very long extension, which gives its snout a conical appearance.

The scales are fairly large for a salmonid and the tail fin deeply forked. The body is completely lacking in spots or other markings. All the fins are grey and the pectoral, pelvic and anal fins are slightly darker at the tip.

Breeding behaviour and life cycle

The houting is an anadromous form of powan and during September and October shoals accumulate in the estuaries of the spawning rivers. When water conditions are suitable, ideally clearing and falling after a spate, shoals move upstream to spawn in shallow, streamy, gravel-bottomed riffles. Powan that live in lakes move inshore during November and December to shoal over extensive gravel banks where they later spawn. In those arctic and subarctic rivers that have powan populations, there is a movement upstream to gravel-bottomed spawning areas.

The freshwater powan spawns at night between late December and February. Several males will consort with ripe females, fertilising their eggs as they shed them. Unlike other salmonids no nest is cut in the gravel. Instead the heavy eggs fall onto the bottom, lodging between the gravel fragments. The eggs have a slightly sticky covering and this prevents them from being washed away. The eggs are large, averaging 2.5mm in diameter, and yellow. Small female powan, often found in deep glacial lakes, may produce as few as 2000, but some large river powan and sea-run houting may produce 20,000.

The eggs hatch after about 13 weeks, the 9–11mm larvae feeding initially on the contents of their yolk sacs before turning to a diet of plankton or minute bottom invertebrates.

Houting fry move quickly downstream to brackish water and eventually the open sea. The fry of lake powan move into deeper water soon after hatching. And river powan fry remain feeding on and around their natal gravel beds before moving into deep water at the onset of winter.

Food and feeding behaviour

River forms feed mainly on small insects, but will rise to take a hatch of flies at the surface, or a fall of land-bred insects. Sea-run houting and lake powan primarily feed on zooplankton, but they will take some food from the bottom, again usually tiny crustaceans, but powan also eat midge larvae and pupae. Zooplankton usually has a marked diurnal movement, rising higher in the water at night and sinking deeper by day – the shoals of feeding powan follow this movement.

Growth and longevity

In oligotrophic lakes and Arctic rivers powan may grow to 10cm after one year, 15cm after two years and 25cm after three years, when the fish are mature. Few live beyond five years, with a maximum length of about 30cm and weight of 350g. In more productive northern lakes exceptionally large fish have been reported at lengths of 70cm and weights of up to 8kg. Adult houting average 30–35cm and 400–550g.

The powan exhibits the characteristic common to all whitefish: a whitish coloration.

Predators

The chief predators in lakes are pike and 'ferox' trout, although some might be taken by birds such as goosanders when they are in shallow spawning areas. River populations are vulnerable to many predators: large trout, pike, arctic terns and goosanders. Houting face the full range of marine predators: seals, seabirds and fish, such as cod.

Conservation status of powan

Many lake populations, especially where the lake is surrounded by rich farmland or there is a large town on its banks, are under threat from eutrophication. In at least two British lakes, the introduction of the ruffe, which devours powan eggs, threatens the powan population (see pages 16–19). Pollution or damming of the lower reaches of rivers draining into the North Sea have probably completely exterminated the North Sea population of houting and some Baltic rivers have lost their stocks for the same reasons. This is a fish species urgently in need of protection throughout the whole of Europe.

Vendace _Coregonus albula_

_This small, herring-like species of whitefish is mainly an
inhabitant of deep, clean lakes where it feeds in shoals.
It is widespread throughout northern Europe also,
occurring in some Baltic rivers._

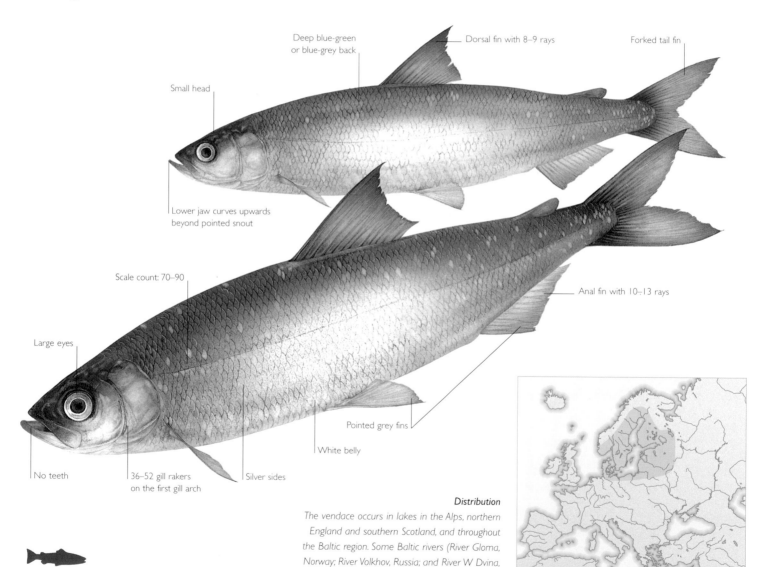

Deep blue-green or blue-grey back

Dorsal fin with 8–9 rays

Forked tail fin

Small head

Lower jaw curves upwards beyond pointed snout

Scale count: 70–90

Anal fin with 10–13 rays

Large eyes

No teeth

36–52 gill rakers on the first gill arch

Silver sides

White belly

Pointed grey fins

c.20cm

Distribution

_The vendace occurs in lakes in the Alps, northern
England and southern Scotland, and throughout
the Baltic region. Some Baltic rivers (River Gloma,
Norway; River Volkhov, Russia; and River W Dvina,
Latvia) have populations of vendace._

The vendace is a slender, streamlined little fish, with a small head, pointed snout and large eyes. Its lower jaw curves upwards and extends slightly beyond the snout so that the mouth opens on the upper side of the snout. This is a diagnostic characteristic and usually makes it easy to separate vendace from powan and pollan. However, as in the mouth structure of some isolated powan populations, this is a variable characteristic and not easy to distinguish in some lakes.

The mouth is toothless; the body is covered with large scales. The adipose fin is distinct; the dorsal, pectoral, pelvic and anal fins are pointed; and the tail fin is forked. The back is deep blue-green or blue-grey, the sides are silver and the belly is white. There are no spots or other markings. The fins are a translucent grey and often darker and opaque at the tips.

Breeding behaviour and life cycle

Vendace shoals move from their deep-water feeding areas in late autumn to shallow water spawning areas where the lake bed is gravel or boulders. It is thought that males arrive before females and between late November and December spawning occurs. Vendace probably do not pair. Instead they appear to remain in shoals: eggs and milt are shed together in the open water. It is therefore likely that the eggs of one female will be fertilised by sperm from several males and that the sperm from one male will fertilise the eggs of several females. The eggs, which are denser than water, sink quickly, falling into cavities between the stones.

Most female vendace are small fish and produce an average of only 3000, 2mm-diameter, yellow eggs. Some large female vendace from Lake Ladoga produce up to 20,000 eggs. The eggs hatch after 13 to 15 weeks and after exhausting their yolk sacs the 8mm young fry disperse and begin to feed on microscopic plankton.

Food and feeding behaviour

The vast majority of food eaten by vendace consists of planktonic crustaceans, especially cladocerans such as *Bosmina, Daphnia* and *Bythotrephes*. These members of the zooplankton feed on diatoms in the phytoplankton, which move vertically during the day in response to light intensity. At midnight, for example, phytoplankton and zooplankton are close to the surface, but as dawn breaks they move deeper, often many metres deeper, in clear lakes. By early afternoon, when sunlight is at its most intense, they are far below the surface, but as the sun goes down they gradually move up again through the water. On overcast days, the migration is not as strong as it is on bright, sunny days. Shoals of feeding vendace follow this vertical migration, filtering the plankton with their gill rakers.

Plankton densities fluctuate widely through the year, with a first flush in April usually reaching a peak in May to June followed by a population crash, but with a second peak in late summer and autumn that is quickly followed by a winter low. Spawning takes place when food supplies are at their lowest, but as there is at least one summer period when plankton foods are scarce, the vendace turns to eating midge pupae that are moving up through the water to hatch at the surface. Occasionally they will also eat flies that have landed on the water surface. In early spring and late autumn, when mid-water food populations are small, vendace have been known to take bottom foods, such as snails, pea-mussels and midge larvae, in some lakes.

Whitefish, such as vendace, are usually found feeding in lakes in shoals. Their small, toothless mouths are perfectly adapted for feeding on the tiny planktonic animals present in the water.

Growth and longevity

The vendace is a small fish, growing to 10cm at the end of the first year, to 18cm at the end of the second year and 20cm after the third year. It matures when two or three years' old. It rarely exceeds 25cm in length, but some have grown to 35cm and 1.2kg in Lake Ladoga.

Predators

Large 'ferox' trout, pike and perch are the main predators of this deep-water fish, although some fish-eating diving birds may well exploit spawning shoals in shallower water.

> ### Conservation status of vendace
> *Eutrophication of lakes has led to the extinction of two Scottish populations and threatens others in British and alpine lakes. With the exception of most Baltic populations, which are thriving and sometimes exploited by commercial fisheries, this is an endangered fish and in need of careful protection.*

Pollan *Coregonus autumnalis*

Until the 1980s the Irish pollan was considered to be a form of the vendace. It has since been identified for certain as being the same species of whitefish that occurs in parts of Arctic Siberia and Canada.

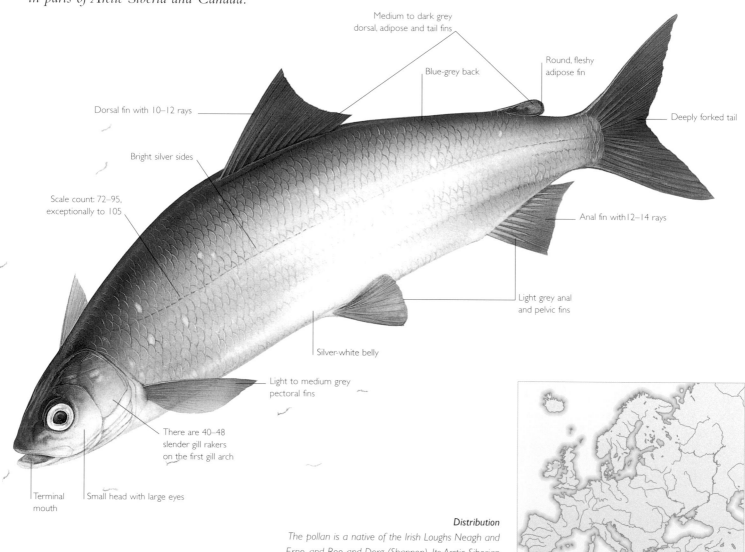

Medium to dark grey dorsal, adipose and tail fins

Round, fleshy adipose fin

Blue-grey back

Dorsal fin with 10–12 rays

Deeply forked tail

Bright silver sides

Scale count: 72–95, exceptionally to 105

Anal fin with 12–14 rays

Light grey anal and pelvic fins

Silver-white belly

Light to medium grey pectoral fins

There are 40–48 slender gill rakers on the first gill arch

Terminal mouth

Small head with large eyes

c.25cm

Distribution
The pollan is a native of the Irish Loughs Neagh and Erne, and Ree and Derg (Shannon). Its Arctic Siberian population might just reach into Arctic European Russia, but this requires further research and clarification.

With its slender, streamlined, slightly laterally flattened body, the pollan closely resembles the other two European whitefish, the powan and vendace. It has a small head, large eyes, a terminal mouth and jaws of equal length. The fins are all pointed, with the exception of the round adipose fin, and the tail fin is deeply forked.

The back is blue-grey, the sides are bright silver, and the belly is silver-white. The dorsal, adipose and tail fins are medium to dark grey, the pectorals are light to medium grey, and the pelvic and anal fins are very light grey.

Breeding behaviour and life cycle

In Lough Neagh spawning takes place in late November and December over shallow water gravel banks. The pollan do not appear to pair and do not cut redds like most salmonids. Instead the eggs are shed and fertilised in mid-water and because they are heavier than water they quickly sink to the bottom.

Each female produces about 3,000–6000, 2mm-diameter, yellow eggs. Three Lough Neagh females, 22–28cm long, contained between 3800 and 5700 eggs. The eggs hatch after about 12 weeks and the 7–8mm young quickly exhaust the remains of food in their yolk sacs before feeding pelagically on microscopic zooplankton.

Food and feeding behaviour

The majority of food in Lough Neagh is taken in mid-water and the pollan's diet is dominated by planktonic crustaceans and midge larvae and pupae. Crustaceans include *Daphnia*, *Bythotrephes*, *Cyclops* and ostracods, and the opossum shrimp *Mysis relicta*, which is, as the pollan, an 'Ice Age relict' species. Midges are among the most abundant benthic invertebrates in Lough Neagh and pollan take midge pupae as they rise to the surface to hatch. During a big evening hatch in summer they will also rise to take adult midges from the water surface.

Between late October and March small planktonic crustacean populations in Lough Neagh collapse and hatches of midges decline. The pollan then seek more food from the lake bed, including the freshwater shrimp *Gammarus*.

A similar pattern of foods and feeding appears to occur in other pollan populations. Lough Neagh also has a huge roach population and it is usual to find feeding roach and pollan shoals intermingling and caught in the same pollan nets.

Growth and longevity

After the first year pollan average about 10cm in length and range from 15 to 20cm after their second year, when the larger specimens may become sexually mature and spawn for the first time. After three years pollan average about 25cm and 30cm after four years. It is known that some pollan live for up to seven years and thought that some may reach 10 years. However, ageing pollan by reading scales is difficult with older fish because pollan lose their scales very easily, and in older fish most of the scales may be replacements, carrying no record of earlier years.

Predators

Perch feed on pollan fry, pike feed on adult pollan – both species have been introduced to the Irish pollan lake. Lough Neagh also has one special pollan predator, a unique form of trout known as the 'dollaghan', which spawns in rivers draining into the lough. This trout can grow to over 10kg (see Conservation status of pollan box).

Note on curious Ice Age relict distributions

It might seem unbelievable to have a fish, the pollan, with its main distribution in western Arctic Canada and Asiatic Siberia with isolated populations in a very few Irish lakes. Yet there are other examples of such incredible distribution involving lakes in the British Isles. For example, the opossum shrimp, *Mysis relicta*, occurs widely in Arctic lakes, in one English lake, Ennerdale (where it may now be extinct) and five Irish lakes. And one species of caddisfly, *Agrypnia crassicornis*, occurs in Mongolia, some lakes in Finland, in one English lake (Malham Tarn) and nowhere else in between!

At one time following the last Ice Age, all these relict species would have been far more widespread. However, in the intervening years, these species have become extinct in between the places where relict populations now exist. The reason for such extinctions can only be surmised, but probably include environmental change (such as warming of lakes and rivers) and competition from other species that were better able to exploit the changing environment.

Related species

The inconnu or White salmon (Stenodus leucichthys) is a typical whitefish with a grey back, silvery sides and a white belly. Its large, overslung mouth helps distinguish it from Atlantic salmon fresh from the sea. Also, it usually has 12–16 rays in its long-based anal fin (the Atlantic salmon has 8–11). There are 19–23 gill rakers on the first gill arch (15–20 in salmon). This predatory whitefish grows large on its fish diet, averaging 50–60cm long and 2–4kg in weight. Inconnu of over 20kg have been reported from Asiatic Siberia and Alaska. Only just a European species, the inconnu occurs in rivers flowing into the Arctic Ocean from the eastern end of the White Sea eastwards. Some live in rivers; others live at sea returning to the rivers to spawn. A rare form of inconnu has been recorded in the Caspian Sea and some rivers draining into the Caspian.

Conservation status of pollan

Over the course of the last 30 years there has been concern about the increasing eutrophication of Lough Neagh. Organic pollution of rivers draining into the lake resulted in a decline of this species and the near extinction of the dollaghan trout that feeds on pollan. Recently, the rivers have become cleaner and the pollan seems to be thriving in the lough as it is currently supporting a large commercial net fishery. The lough and its rivers are now carefully monitored. Pollan still survive in Lough Erne, although whether it is thriving or not is not clearly known. The species is now probably extinct in the Shannon loughs through over-eutrophication (an attempt to trace them in 1988 was unsuccessful).

Grayling *Thymallus thymallus*

The grayling is not only a beautiful fish and a popular catch for anglers, it is also the best indicator of clean water among all European freshwater fish.

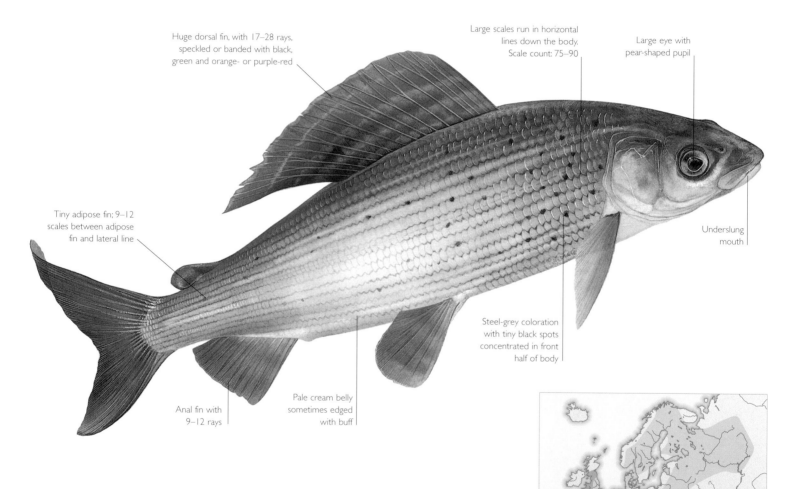

Huge dorsal fin, with 17–28 rays, speckled or banded with black, green and orange- or purple-red

Large scales run in horizontal lines down the body. Scale count: 75–90

Large eye with pear-shaped pupil

Tiny adipose fin; 9–12 scales between adipose fin and lateral line

Underslung mouth

Anal fin with 9–12 rays

Pale cream belly sometimes edged with buff

Steel-grey coloration with tiny black spots concentrated in front half of body

← c.35cm →

Distribution
The grayling occurs in clean rivers throughout much of northern and eastern Europe. It has been introduced to many rivers that never held grayling or where grayling were wiped out by pollution. It also occurs in clean lakes, especially in Fenno-Scandinavia and northern Russia. Unlike salmonids, grayling cannot live in seawater.

Spawning grayling: two males have joined the one female and together they ensure 100 per cent fertilisation of her eggs.

Although it has its own family, *thymallidae*, the presence of an adipose fin and its slender, streamlined build indicate that the grayling is not too distantly related to the salmonids. It has a huge dorsal fin, large scales arranged in lines running down its body, a distinctly underslung mouth and pear-shaped pupils. The dorsal fin is speckled or banded with black, green and orange- or purple-red; all the other fins are predominantly grey. Younger fish tend to be more silvery and very aged specimens are much darker, almost black. In the limestone streams of southeastern Europe grayling are much paler, a light creamy-brown often with apricot fins.

Breeding behaviour and life cycle

Grayling spawn between March and May in fast, shallow water over small gravel in rivers or in shallow water (20–60cm deep) in gravel-bottomed lake margins. The female cuts a redd into which she sheds a batch of yellow-orange, 4mm-diameter eggs. Each female produces about 3000 eggs per kilogram of her body weight. After fertilisation, the female covers the eggs with gravel.

Hatching occurs after 20 to 35 days, depending on water temperature. Newly hatched grayling, 10–12mm long, remain in the redd for only three to 10 days before the yolk sacs are exhausted and they must swim up to open water to seek food.

Mortality among grayling in their first year is highly variable. Hot summers with low river levels and low oxygen levels can result in the majority of a year's production dying. Heavy losses can also occur in autumn and winter as it seems young fish cannot withstand huge spates as older, larger fish can. It is not unusual, therefore, to find one or two 'year classes' completely missing in a river grayling population. It is also not unusual, following three or four bad years, for the grayling population in a river to seem close to extinction, but after one or two good years, the population recovers and is as abundant as ever.

Food and feeding behaviour

Most food is obtained from the river or lake bed and consists of whatever small invertebrates are present, such as stonefly nymphs, midge larvae and pupae, freshwater shrimps, small snails and aquatic worms. During a hatch of water-bred flies or a fall of land-bred flies, grayling will feed at the surface. Trout feeding in this way usually lie 'on the fin' just beneath the surface and take every fly that passes, whereas grayling always rise from the bottom and take only one insect each time they rise.

Small- to medium-sized grayling are strictly shoal fish and prefer to lie in open water rather than split the shoal up around intervening boulders or weeds. Shoals will sometimes move from pool to pool in search of food. Larger grayling may also shoal, usually in separate shoals from smaller fish, but they are sometimes solitary or occur in twos or threes. They are often found in deeper, more turbulent water than shoals of smaller grayling.

Growth and longevity

Grayling generally grow rapidly. In the southern Alps they average 12.2cm after one year, 27.7cm after two years and 34.9cm after three years. Here few grayling live for more than four to five years and have grown as long as 46cm. In England growth is slower with averages of 10.2cm after one year, 20.7cm after two years and 27.9cm after three years. Here some grayling live for eight to nine years and measure 40–42cm. Farther north, in Lapland, growth is even slower, but the grayling live for much longer, with some living for 10 to 12 years and growing to lengths of up to 52cm. Most adult grayling weigh 400–750g, and occasional fish of more than 1.5kg are exceptional.

Predators

In southeast Europe marbled trout (see pages 52–53) and huchen (see pages 54–55) are major predators. Elsewhere, such as in Austrian rivers, an increase of the cormorant population has been blamed for a massive decline in grayling stocks.

Conservation status of grayling

Generally this is an abundant fish and is one whose population usually recovers rapidly following a one-off pollution incident. Until fairly recently it was considered vermin in some rivers on the grounds that it competed with trout and salmon parr and it was ruthlessly destroyed. However, several studies have demonstrated that there is no competition between grayling and brown trout or that, where there is, brown trout is the dominant species. Grayling persecution has consequently been reduced.

Smelt *Osmerus eperlanus*

The smelt, a distant relative of the salmonids, is primarily a marine fish that spawns in rivers, but there are a few landlocked lake populations.

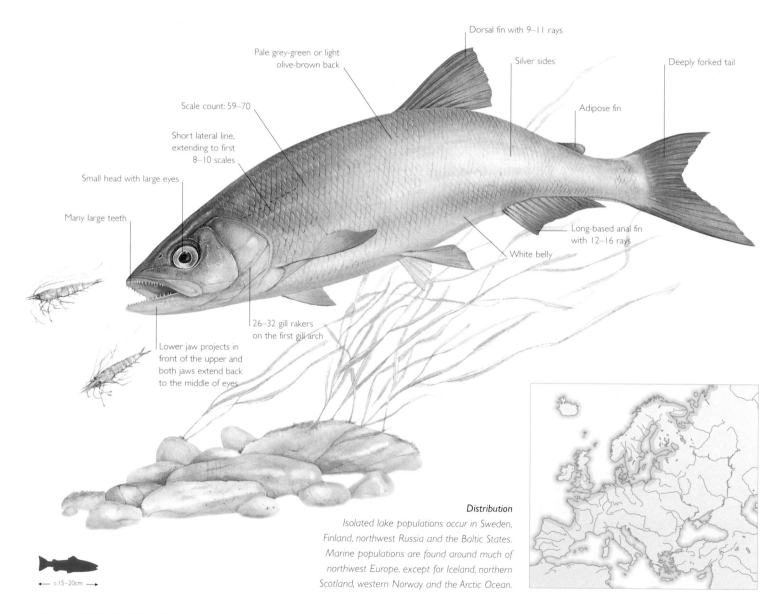

Dorsal fin with 9–11 rays

Silver sides

Deeply forked tail

Pale grey-green or light olive-brown back

Adipose fin

Scale count: 59–70

Short lateral line, extending to first 8–10 scales

Small head with large eyes

Many large teeth

Long-based anal fin with 12–16 rays

White belly

Lower jaw projects in front of the upper and both jaws extend back to the middle of eyes

26–32 gill rakers on the first gill arch

c.15–20cm

Distribution

Isolated lake populations occur in Sweden, Finland, northwest Russia and the Baltic States. Marine populations are found around much of northwest Europe, except for Iceland, northern Scotland, western Norway and the Arctic Ocean.

Identified as a very distant relative of the salmonids by its tiny adipose fin and slender trout-like build, the smelt can easily be confused with the whitefish (see pages 64–69). It has a small head, large, conspicuous eyes, the lower jaw projects beyond the upper and both jaws extend back as far as the middle of the eye (to the rear of the eye in marine populations). It has large, numerous teeth. The anal fin is long-based and the tail fin is deeply forked. The lateral line appears short, extending as far as the first eight to 10 scales.

Overall coloration is a translucent silver in live smelts. The back is pale grey-green or olive-brown, the sides are silver and the belly is white. Surprisingly, this fish smells strongly of cucumber.

Breeding behaviour and life cycle

Marine smelts enter the lower freshwater reaches of rivers in March and April and mating occurs immediately on arrival. The little fish swim excitedly in shoals in a sexual frenzy, the females scattering their eggs, which are immediately fertilised by accompanying males. Small, first-time spawning females (the majority) produce about 10,000 eggs; older larger smelts produce up to 40,000.

The outer membrane of the small, 1mm-diameter eggs, which are yellow when laid but become transparent after fertilisation, is sticky. This membrane bursts to form a stalk, which sticks the egg to sand, gravel or vegetation. Sometimes they are scattered in very shallow water and, should the water level fall, they are left stranded. Often the stalk breaks and the remains act like a drogue, holding the drifting egg in the current.

The eggs hatch after three to five weeks and the 6mm-long fry begin to eat planktonic organisms as they drift downstream to the estuary. Many adults die during and after spawning; those that survive swim immediately back to saltwater.

Lake forms of smelt may migrate to inflowing streams to spawn or remain in the lake to spawn over lake shallows in March to May.

Food and feeding behaviour

Young smelts eat plankton, which they filter from the water with their gill rakers. Plankton continues to be a major source of food for lake populations, although larger fish will also eat lake-bed invertebrates, such as freshwater shrimps and caddis larvae. Sea-going smelts feed on larger crustaceans, such as shrimps, small crabs, mysids and palaemonids, and the small fry of sprats, herrings and flounders.

Feeding activity in marine smelt is largely regulated by the tidal and diurnal cycles. Shoals of smelt feed keenly as the tide floods and ebbs, and feed most keenly on tides that peak after dusk or before dawn.

Growth and longevity

Smelts have a slow growth rate. Lake smelts mature at two years of age when they measure up to 10cm long. Female sea-going smelts grow to about 10cm after one year, 12–15cm after two years and 15–18cm after three years, when many breed for the first time. Others wait another year before they breed. Many do not survive spawning, but those that do reach a maximum length of 18–20cm and maximum age of five to six years. Males tend to be about 75 per cent of the size of females of the same age.

Predators

Divers and grebes eat smelts during winter, terns eat them in summer and cormorants and red-breasted mergansers eat them throughout

With the exception of several lake populations, smelt tend to be saltwater shoal fish that enter estuaries in order to spawn.

the year. Among the smelt's fish predators are the sea trout, the sea-run form of brown trout (see pages 50–51) and sea bass, which have been recorded gorging on smelts in northwest European estuaries.

Conservation status of smelt

Because this species requires clean estuaries for feeding and clean, freshwater reaches immediately upstream of the tide for spawning, it has been exterminated in many rivers because of gross pollution. It has also been lost in some rivers through damming immediately above the tide. From 1900–60 smelt populations were at their lowest in estuaries around the coastline of industrialised Europe, but in recent years the cleaning up of rivers has seen the smelt reappearing in many areas. In some clean rivers there is a viable commercial fishery. The Rostherne Mere population, England's only landlocked, entirely freshwater population of smelt, died out during the 1920s through over-eutrophication of the lake.

Chub *Leuciscus cephalus*

The chub is one of the most widespread European river fish – shoals occur in the deep pools of lowland reaches to the shallow pools of the grayling zone. A powerful fish, the chub has long been a favourite among anglers.

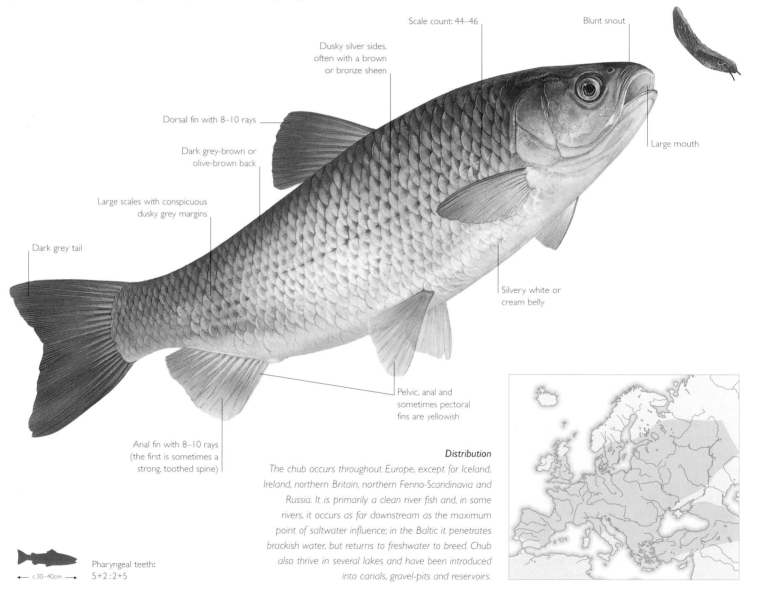

Scale count: 44–46

Dusky silver sides, often with a brown or bronze sheen

Blunt snout

Dorsal fin with 8–10 rays

Large mouth

Dark grey-brown or olive-brown back

Large scales with conspicuous dusky grey margins

Dark grey tail

Silvery white or cream belly

Pelvic, anal and sometimes pectoral fins are yellowish

Anal fin with 8–10 rays (the first is sometimes a strong, toothed spine)

c.30–40cm

Pharyngeal teeth: 5+2 : 2+5

Distribution

The chub occurs throughout Europe, except for Iceland, Ireland, northern Britain, northern Fenno-Scandinavia and Russia. It is primarily a clean river fish and, in some rivers, it occurs as far downstream as the maximum point of saltwater influence; in the Baltic it penetrates brackish water, but returns to freshwater to breed. Chub also thrive in several lakes and have been introduced into canals, gravel-pits and reservoirs.

The chub is a moderately slender species with a wide, blunt-snouted head, large mouth, broad shoulders and a stout tail. The pelvic fin base is anterior to the front of the dorsal fin base and the free edges of the dorsal and anal fins are distinctly convex. Lateral line scale counts and pharyngeal teeth examinations may be necessary to confirm separation of *Leuciscus* species.

During the breeding season the male grows small tubercles on his head and shoulders.

Breeding behaviour and life cycle

Shoals of adult chub move from their deep-water winter lies in late April to early May and head for gravel-bottomed, rapid shallows. There may be a long upstream migration, sometimes 30km or more. Lake populations move onto gravel-bottomed, shallow margins or feeder streams.

Chub are communal breeders, several males joining a female that is ready to spawn. Each female produces 40,000–50,000, 1mm-diameter, yellow or pale orange eggs per kilogram of her own body weight. These are laid in May to June on the bottom or among weeds and the sticky eggs adhere to gravel or weed. The 4–5mm larvae hatch eight to 14 days after fertilisation and, a few days later when their yolk sacs are exhausted, the tiny fry move into the shallowest margins. Here they feed on particles of organic detritus, algae and tiny invertebrates, before turning to the adult diet.

Adults return downstream much more slowly than their upstream migration, often remaining in the shallow spawning stretches until late autumn. Lake populations move to deeper water soon after spawning is over.

Food and feeding behaviour

Chub eat a wide variety of aquatic invertebrates, including caddis larvae and stonefly nymphs taken from the river or lake bed, nymphs and pupae rising to hatch, and adult insects on the water surface. When a river is in spate, chub will also take slugs, earthworms and insect larvae washed into the river; when a river has burst its banks, shoals will swim over flooded pastures to take drowned earthworms and slugs. In autumn, they will eat fruits and seeds that fall into the water. Large chub will also eat small amphibians and fish, including the fry of trout, grayling and their own species.

Unlike many cyprinids, chub will feed in most weather conditions. In high summer, when water temperatures are high, they feed between dusk and dawn. In winter they will feed at water temperatures down to 3–4°C, usually in deep pools, from mid-afternoon to well after dark.

Growth and longevity

In most European rivers, chub growth is slow. They grow to 5cm after one year, 10cm or more after two years, 15cm or more after three years and 20–25cm after four to five years when the fish mature (females usually mature a year later than males). Most chub might grow to an average maximum length of about 40cm, weighing up to 2kg. Lengths of up to 1m, weights of up to 7.25kg and ages of 10 to 12 years are exceptional.

Predators

Small chub are prey for a wide variety of fish predators, which include pike, and birds, such as herons. Otters and cormorants tend to eat larger specimens.

Related species

The Black Sea chub (Leuciscus borysthenicus) resembles a small chub, but its dorsal and anal fins are straight or only slightly concave. It sometimes has a darkish band extending forwards from its tail along either side of the body. The scale count along the lateral line is diagnostic: 36–40. After three years most Black Sea chub are up to 9cm long. A fish of 25cm is a specimen, while fish measuring 30cm or more are exceptional. This species occurs in the lower reaches of rivers flowing into the Black Sea only.

Conservation status of chub

This species is one of the most abundant European river fish. It is currently being reintroduced to rivers where it was exterminated by pollution, but that are now capable of sustaining a fish population.

Rudd *Scardinius erythrophthalmus*

Often confused with the roach, the rudd is a more strikingly colourful fish. It feeds on midges at the water surface — rings and dimples made by feeding rudd are a familiar sight in a weedy mere on a summer's evening.

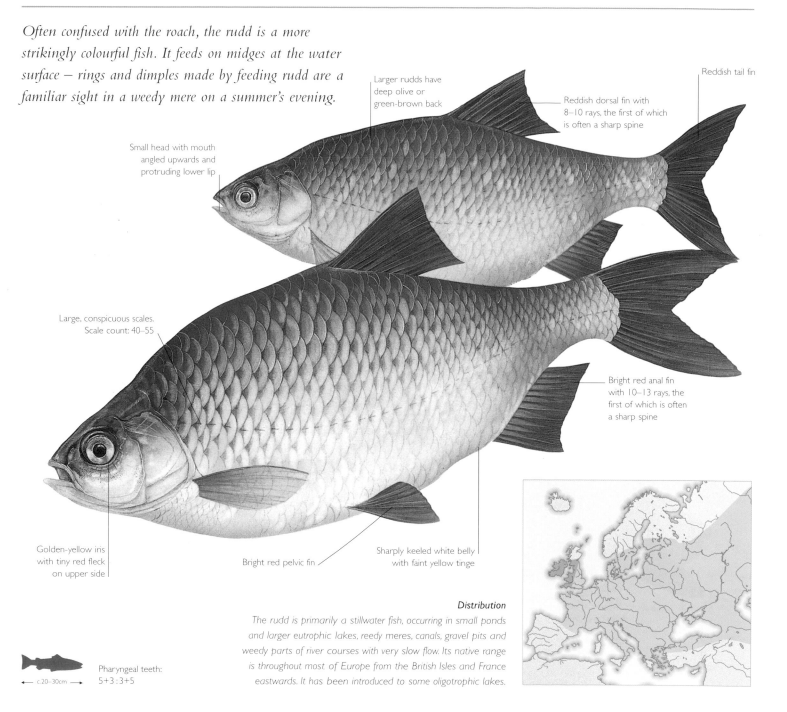

Larger rudds have deep olive or green-brown back

Reddish dorsal fin with 8–10 rays, the first of which is often a sharp spine

Reddish tail fin

Small head with mouth angled upwards and protruding lower lip

Large, conspicuous scales. Scale count: 40–55

Bright red anal fin with 10–13 rays, the first of which is often a sharp spine

Golden-yellow iris with tiny red fleck on upper side

Bright red pelvic fin

Sharply keeled white belly with faint yellow tinge

c 20–30cm

Pharyngeal teeth: 5+3 : 3+5

Distribution

The rudd is primarily a stillwater fish, occurring in small ponds and larger eutrophic lakes, reedy meres, canals, gravel pits and weedy parts of river courses with very slow flow. Its native range is throughout most of Europe from the British Isles and France eastwards. It has been introduced to some oligotrophic lakes.

The rudd is one of Europe's most common fish and, for many, one of the most beautiful.

8–12cm after one or two years, with a maximum of up to 35cm, weighing up to 800g, at eight to 10 years old. In exceptional cases, rudd can grow to 45cm and weigh up to 2kg. Few live for longer than 10 years.

Predators
Perch and herons are probably the major predators of tiny rudd, while pike are the main, and perhaps the only, predator of large rudd in weedy lowland lakes.

Related species
The Greek rudd (Scardinius graecus) is a more slender bodied fish than the rudd and has a small, more flattened head. Coloration is similar to that of the rudd: the body is olive-brown on the back shading to silvery sides, often with a yellow cast, and a white belly. The pectoral, anal and pelvic fins are red in colour. Fin ray and scale counts are within the range of the rudd. The Greek rudd occurs only in Lakes Yliki and Paralimni in eastern Greece and it may be better to consider this a subspecies of the rudd.

The Acheloos rudd (Scardinius acarnanicus) is not as slender as the Greek rudd and not as deep in the body as the rudd. As in the rudd, the mouth is upturned. The pectoral, pelvic and anal fins are dark with just a slight reddish tinge. Fin ray and scale counts are within the range of the rudd. This species occurs only in Lakes Trichonis and Lyssimachia and the Acheloos river system of western Greece. It too may be better considered a subspecies of the rudd.

Conservation status of rudd
This is an often abundant fish, especially in very shallow waters. If roach are present they will usually greatly outnumber rudd.

The rudd is a deep-bodied fish, usually with more laterally flattened sides than the roach and with a sharply keeled belly between the pelvic and anal fins. The head is small, the mouth is angled upwards and the lower lip protrudes beyond the upper lip. The front of the dorsal fin base is farther back on the body than the base of the pelvic fin (see roach on pages 92–93).

Small rudds are generally silvery, but larger rudds are more colourful. The big scales are very conspicuous. All fins are usually reddish; the pelvic and anal fins are a bright blood-red (these are visible in peaty water when the rest of the fish is hidden). Some rudd do have bright lemon-yellow fins and specimens of this colour morph can be found in shoals of fish with the usual fin colour. The iris is golden-yellow with a tiny red fleck on the upper side, never all-red.

Beware of the following hybrids (see pages 140–41): rudd × roach, rudd × dace, rudd × bream, rudd × silver bream and rudd × bleak.

Breeding behaviour and life cycle
The rudd spawns in April and May among weed beds or at the edge of emergent reeds or sedges along river or lake margin. The 1–1.5mm-diameter, pale yellow, sticky eggs are attached to the weeds, often by the female holding her vent against the weeds as she sheds them. Several males may fertilise the eggs. Each female produces an equivalent of about 10,000 per 100g of body weight; stunted females may produce as few as 6000, very large females up 200,000. The eggs hatch after three to 15 days, depending on water temperature, and the larval rudd remain attached to weeds for a further three to seven days until their yolk sacs have been absorbed. They then form shoals and feed on tiny planktonic organisms.

Like many species that spawn in shallow water in spring, if water levels fall quickly, an entire year's egg production may be lost. This often results in some year classes or several year classes missing, when there are a few such springs in succession.

Food and feeding behaviour
Rudd are omnivorous, feeding on algae and aquatic weeds, small seeds and fruits, and invertebrates such as freshwater shrimps, hog-lice, midge larvae and pupae. As in the bleak (see pages 114–15), the rudd's upturned mouth is perhaps an adaptation for feeding at the water surface. During an evening midge hatch the entire rudd population of a lake might rise to feed.

Growth and longevity
In small ponds, rudd will often be stunted with an average length of 8–12cm. In big lakes where food is more plentiful, they grow to approximately

Bitterling *Rhodeus sericeus*

The bitterling is a lovely little fish with one of the most remarkable and unique reproductive cycles in the piscatorial world.

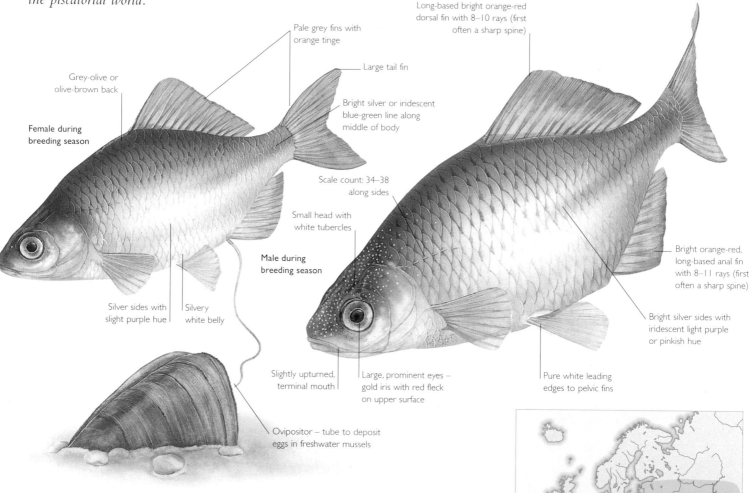

Long-based bright orange-red dorsal fin with 8–10 rays (first often a sharp spine)

Pale grey fins with orange tinge

Large tail fin

Grey-olive or olive-brown back

Bright silver or iridescent blue-green line along middle of body

Female during breeding season

Scale count: 34–38 along sides

Small head with white tubercles

Male during breeding season

Bright orange-red, long-based anal fin with 8–11 rays (first often a sharp spine)

Silver sides with slight purple hue

Silvery white belly

Bright silver sides with iridescent light purple or pinkish hue

Slightly upturned, terminal mouth

Large, prominent eyes – gold iris with red fleck on upper surface

Pure white leading edges to pelvic fins

Ovipositor – tube to deposit eggs in freshwater mussels

c.6cm

Pharyngeal teeth: 5 : 5

Distribution

The bitterling is widespread throughout Europe from northeastern France eastwards, but they are absent from the north and Italy. It lives in small, very weedy lakes, ponds and canals, and occasionally deep, slow reaches of lowland rivers with extensive weed beds. As well as weed, the other essential ingredient of the bitterling habitat is the presence of freshwater mussels.

The bitterling is a very small fish with a laterally compressed, but moderately deep body that humps slightly at the front edge of the dorsal fin. The scales are large. The dorsal and anal fins are fairly long-based and proportionally quite large for the size of the fish, as is the tail fin. The lateral line is short, extending over only the first five to six scales from the rear of the gill cover.

Coloration is grey-olive or olive-brown back, silver sides with a light purple or pinkish hue and a silvery white belly. There is a bright silver or iridescent blue-green streak along the midline of the body between the anal and tail fins. The fins are pale grey with a slight orange tinge. The iris is gold with a red fleck on the upper surface.

During the breeding season the males have brighter, more iridescent silver sides and white tubercles on the head, bright orange-red dorsal and anal fins, and pure enamel-white leading edges to the pelvic fins.

Breeding behaviour and life cycle

Spawning is triggered off in April or May by the presence of freshwater mussels. Experiments have shown that it is actually the sight of mussels that triggers reproduction. The male develops his breeding coloration and the female develops a long egg-depositing tube or ovipositor from her vent. This tube is up to 6cm long, which is equivalent to her body length.

The male selects a mussel that becomes the centre of his territory, which he defends vigorously while looking out for passing females until one that is ready to lay her eggs accepts his invitation to mate. Together they court around the chosen mussel until, when she is ready to lay, her ovipositor stiffens and she inserts it into the gaping mussel. About 25 proportionally large (up to 3.5mm in diameter), very pale yellow eggs are injected into the mantle cavity of the mussel where they stick to the gill. The male then sheds milt, containing sperm, at the entrance of the breathing tube and the mussel inadvertently sucks in the sperm to fertilise the eggs.

A female usually produces up to four batches of eggs, or a maximum of about 100 eggs, which is a very small number for a member of the carp family. However, bitterling eggs are well protected within the mussel.

The eggs hatch after three to four weeks, and two to three days later the 10mm-long bitterling fry swim from the mussel. This is not a one-sided

The relationship between bitterling and mussel is a classic example of a symbiotic association, where two very different species benefit from their association.

affair, however. The bitterling spawning season coincides with the mussel spawning season and mussel larvae (*glochidia*) attach themselves to the skin or gills of the mating bitterling. The adult bitterling then swim away and the mussel larvae eventually detach themselves and sink away from their parents. In this way, the bitterling helps the dispersal and spread of the mussel population.

Food and feeding behaviour

All ages of bitterling browse microscopic algae from boulders and graze silkweed and pondweed. They also eat small invertebrates including aquatic insects larvae, especially midges, and worms. They stop feeding when the water temperature falls below 6–8°C and they spend winter in deep, weedy water in a state of suspended animation.

Growth and longevity

In its first year the bitterling grows from 10mm to 3–4cm and matures at two to three years old when it measures up to 6cm long. In aquaria and garden ponds they have occasionally lived for six years and grown to 8.5cm, but in the wild they rarely live for more than four years.

Predators

Other fish, including pike, perch and zander, are probably the main predators. Although they may be taken by herons in very shallow water, poor visibility in the murky or very weedy water inhabited by the bitterling makes it difficult for birds to see them.

Conservation status of bitterling
Although never abundant in the way that the roach is, the bitterling is numerous throughout its range wherever there are suitable conditions. It is spreading in some areas through weeded canals and has become a popular cold-water aquarium fish.

Minnow *Phoxinus phoxinus*

Vast shoals of this tiny fish are a familiar summer sight to naturalists and anglers, especially in broad, shallow, gravel-bottomed river pools. They are important in the diet of many piscivorous birds and fish.

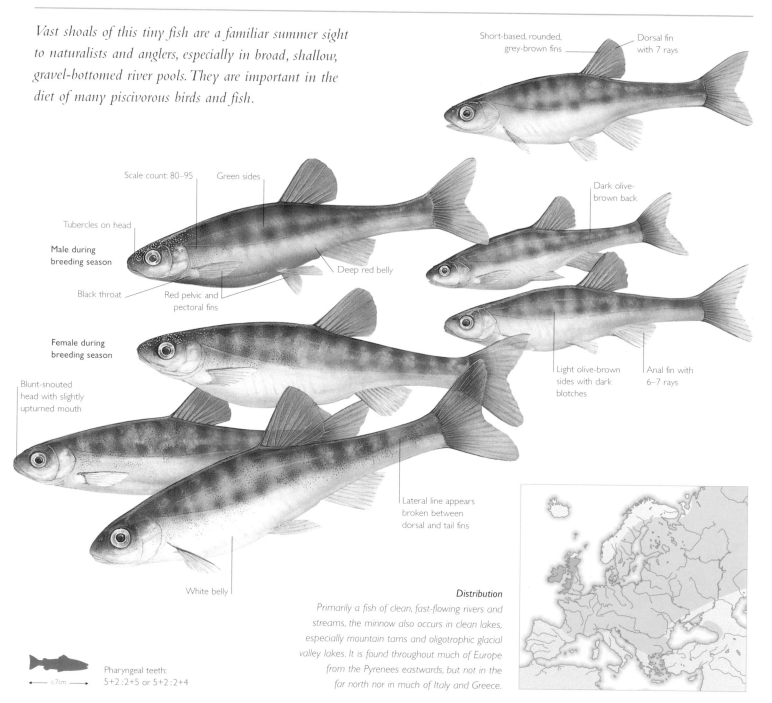

Short-based, rounded, grey-brown fins

Dorsal fin with 7 rays

Scale count: 80–95

Green sides

Tubercles on head

Dark olive-brown back

Male during breeding season

Black throat

Red pelvic and pectoral fins

Deep red belly

Female during breeding season

Light olive-brown sides with dark blotches

Anal fin with 6–7 rays

Blunt-snouted head with slightly upturned mouth

Lateral line appears broken between dorsal and tail fins

White belly

c.7cm

Pharyngeal teeth: 5+2 : 2+5 or 5+2 : 2+4

Distribution

Primarily a fish of clean, fast-flowing rivers and streams, the minnow also occurs in clean lakes, especially mountain tarns and oligotrophic glacial valley lakes. It is found throughout much of Europe from the Pyrenees eastwards, but not in the far north nor in much of Italy and Greece.

The minnow is a very small slender fish with a rounded cross section, a small, blunt-snouted head and a slightly upturned mouth. The fins are all short-based and rounded. The scales are minute, deeply embedded in the skin and difficult to dislodge, and the lateral line appears to be broken between the dorsal and tail fins.

The coloration is a dark olive-brown back, lighter olive-brown sides with a series of darker blotches that are especially conspicuous along the tail, and a white belly. All the fins are grey-brown, but the pelvic and anal fins are paler than the others. Younger fish are lighter in colour and the dark blotches give the illusion of a blackish stripe along the sides as the young minnows dart through shallow water. Breeding males develop tubercles on the head, as do some females, in the spawning season, and bright deep red bellies, green sides, red pectoral and pelvic fins, and blackish throats. It is possible to confuse them with male three-spined sticklebacks at this time (see pages 156–57).

Breeding behaviour and life cycle

As the water warms in early spring, adult minnows that live in rivers gather in shoals in shallow riffles and the tails and necks of pools, usually where there is clean fine gravel. Sometimes shoals will migrate several kilometres upstream to suitable spawning areas, often to shallow water that is less deep than the body of the tiny fish. Lake populations also seek extensive shallows, often the gravel fans formed by inflowing lakes or in shallow bays.

Spawning occurs from May to July and the eggs are deposited in clumps, which stick to the gravel or get washed into cavities in the gravel. Each female produces approximately 1000, 1.2mm-diameter, pale dull yellow eggs, which hatch about five to eight days after fertilisation. The 4–5mm-long larvae remain within the gravel for several more days until their yolk sacs have been fully absorbed. Then, as young fry, they move into the shallowest sunlit margins, sometimes in water that is only 2–5cm deep, often forming huge nursery shoals, where they feed on tiny organic particles, algae and tiny zooplankton.

Food and feeding behaviour

Minnows eat primarily minute river- or lake-bed invertebrates, including blackfly and midge larvae, small stonefly and mayfly nymphs and aquatic worms. They will also rise to take insects from the surface using a form of teamwork. When a large mayfly or daddy-long-legs drifts on the surface overhead, several minnows will rise and grab at the feet and body of the insect. Eventually the relatively huge insect is dragged under and the shoal devours it.

From spring to autumn minnows are shoal fish, but when the temperature drops from late October shoals disperse and the minnow becomes far more solitary. It then seeks deeper pools and hides away under boulders or crannies in a bank. Minnows will continue to take some food unless the water temperature falls to below approximately 4°C.

Growth and longevity

Minnows mature at the end of their first year at 3–4cm long. These first-year fish usually spawn later in the season than older minnows. Most live for a maximum of two to three years and grow to 6–9cm long. Very few live to four or five years; one five-year-old captive specimen reached 12.5cm. Females are larger than males of the same age.

Predators

The minnow is a major summer food for many fish-eating fish including trout, chub, perch and asp. Large river trout will often stop feeding on insects when minnows are close by and will slowly sidle down the river and rush through the shallows, scattering minnow shoals and battering the tiny fish. They will then slowly pick off those that are dead and maimed.

Birds such as the grey heron, kingfisher, goosander, red-breasted merganser, and the common and arctic tern often feed on minnows. So too does the black-headed gull, a species not adept at fishing – it will plunge dive from the air to catch minnows, but fewer than 10 per cent of dives are successful. Dippers are usually regarded as insectivorous birds, but during the late spring

Minnows are one of the most important fodder-fish, providing food for a wide range of other fish and aquatic birds.

and summer they take many minnows, battering them on waterside boulders before swallowing them down whole.

Raising the alarm

Like many shoal fish and herd animals, cyprinids such as the minnow benefit when a predator approaches on the grounds that 'several pairs of eyes are better than one'. Certainly observations indicate that if a potential predator is seen by just one or two fish in the shoal, then the rest of the shoal is immediately made aware of the danger. The way in which they do this is not fully understood. Recent experiments have revealed that shoal cyprinids that have been injured by a predator can warn the rest of the shoal by emitting chemicals from their wounds.

Conservation status of minnow
The minnow is abundant throughout its range. Populations should be closely monitored in every lake system because their existence not only indicates clean water, but they also provide an essential food for many aquatic and waterside animals. Should the minnow population of a river or lake collapse, so too will the whole aquatic ecosystem.

Swamp Minnow *Phoxinus percnurus*

This tiny minnow is almost unknown because of its eastern distribution and very restricted habitat.

The swamp minnow is a slender little fish with a slightly deeper body than the more widespread minnow. Its maximum body depth is at least 25 per cent of its length compared with 20 to 25 per cent in the minnow. The head appears fairly large (and is larger than the minnow's).

Breeding behaviour and life cycle
The swamp minnow spawns in June to early July among dense weed in shallow water. It seems that eggs are deposited in clumps of up to 150 to 200 over several days. Swamp minnows probably mate in small shoals so eggs will be fertilised by sperm from several males. The eggs are 1mm in diameter and very pale grey with a yellow tinge. They hatch after about one week – one clump hatched and the larvae dispersed eight days after being laid.

Food and feeding behaviour
Swamp minnows are shoal fish and will eat any small invertebrate they can swallow, from tiny copepod and cladoceran crustaceans to larger water hog-lice, midge larvae and pupae, and smaller caddis. They will also rise to the surface to take adult midges and insects that have been blown onto the water. One shoal was observed dragging green grasshoppers, which had accidentally jumped onto the pool, under the surface and pulling them apart.

Growth and longevity
There is very little information available, but maximum length is about 10–12cm; exceptionally 15cm. Swamp minnows probably live to a maximum of four or five years.

Predators
Perch and kingfishers are probably the main predators of the swamp minnow.

Distribution and habitat
This species has a very restricted range from Poland eastwards into northern Russia. It occurs in weed-choked pools and river back waters.

Conservation status of swamp minnow
This species is a common, but largely unseen, fish. However, the draining of small weedy pools and the 'tidying up' of weedy lake margins and back waters have been resposible for destroying some populations

---

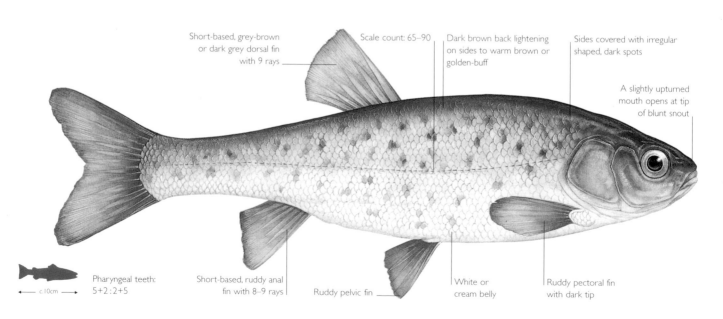

Short-based, grey-brown or dark grey dorsal fin with 9 rays

Scale count: 65–90

Dark brown back lightening on sides to warm brown or golden-buff

Sides covered with irregular shaped, dark spots

A slightly upturned mouth opens at tip of blunt snout

Pharyngeal teeth: 5+2 : 2+5

c.10cm

Short-based, ruddy anal fin with 8–9 rays

Ruddy pelvic fin

White or cream belly

Ruddy pectoral fin with dark tip

Spanish Minnowcarp

Phoxinellus hispanicus

This is one of Europe's least-known fishes. It is tiny, of no economic significance, with a restricted distribution.

Related species
The Guadalquivir minnow (Iberocypris palaciosi) occurs only in Spain's River Guadalquivir. The Dalmatian minnow (Paraphoxinus croaticus) occurs in rivers draining into the Adriatic from southern Slovenia to northern Greece. The Albanian minnow (Pachychilon pictum) is found only in the Skutari and Ohrid catchments of Albania. The false rasbora (Pseudorabora parva) occurs in the Danube system.

Conservation status of Spanish minnowcarp
Three shoals were seen in Guadiana in 1998. Today the Spannish minnowcarp is one of Europe's most endangered animals.

This is a tiny, slender fish with a small head, large eyes and a prominent, upturned lower jaw that makes the mouth slightly superior. The anal and dorsal fins are short-based and the tail fin deeply forked. The back is green-grey, the sides are silvery flecked with yellow in immatures and golden-yellow in spawning adults, and the belly is white. A black stripe separates the dark back from the bright sides.

Breeding behaviour and life cycle
Spanish minnowcarp spawn in May and probably in June in shallow weedy or rocky margins, probably in shoals. It is thought that it lays its eggs in batches. One 5.5mm-long, ripe female netted within a shoal of about 20 fish had 82 developed eggs (about 0.8mm in diameter and pale grey) and others that were undeveloped.

Food and feeding behaviour
The Spanish minnowcarp is a shoal fish that appears to take most of its food from or close to the river bed. The analyses of 11 stomachs one June revealed a diet that is dominated by midge larvae and microscopic algae. The tiny crustaceans, cladocerans, were present in two of the stomachs that were inspected.

Growth and longevity
Little is known about the Spanish minnowcarp, but in May to June one year, 27 specimens from three different shoals had an average length of 5.2cm (with a range of 4.5–6.5cm). There are records of fish measuring 7.5cm. This species' life expectancy is unknown.

Predators
Spanish minnowcarp are probably eaten by larger fish and fish-eating birds, but no study has been carried out.

Distribution and habitat
The Spanish minnowcarp is found only in the Rivers Guadiana and Guadalquivir and their tributaries in southern Portugal and Spain.

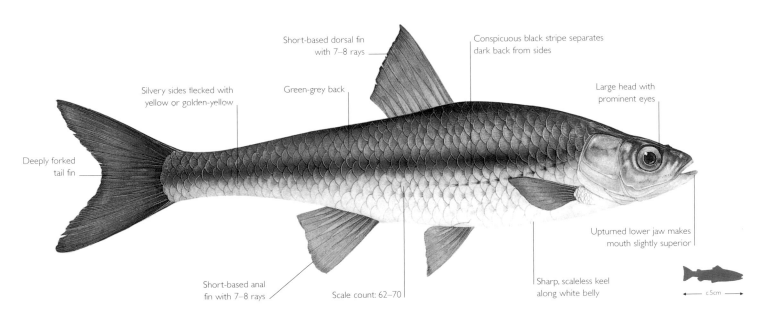

Short-based dorsal fin with 7–8 rays

Conspicuous black stripe separates dark back from sides

Silvery sides flecked with yellow or golden-yellow

Green-grey back

Large head with prominent eyes

Deeply forked tail fin

Upturned lower jaw makes mouth slightly superior

Short-based anal fin with 7–8 rays

Scale count: 62–70

Sharp, scaleless keel along white belly

c.5cm

Bream (Bronze Bream) *Abramis brama*

The bream is a large, 'slab-sided' member of the carp family and an important member of the fish community of lowland shallow meres and canals. It is the slimiest European fish.

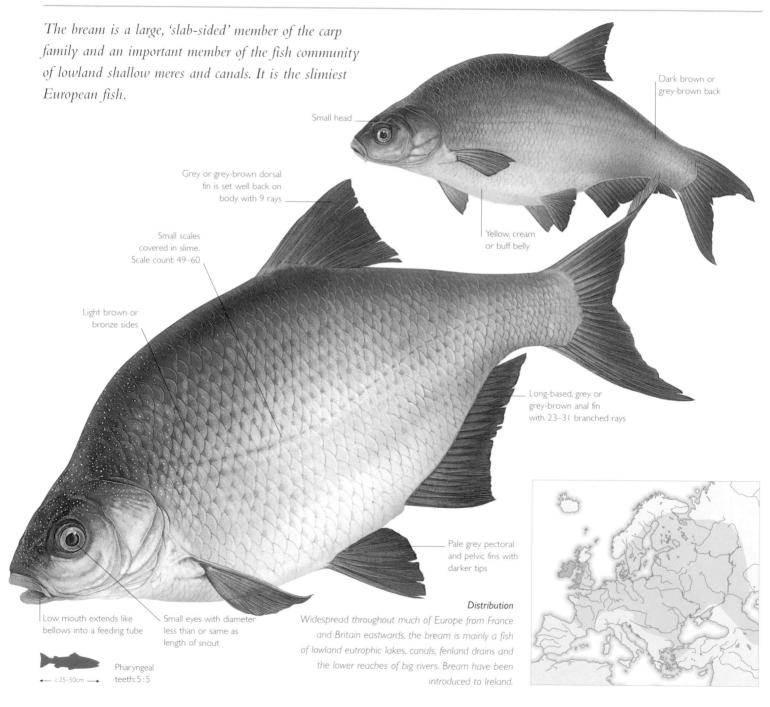

Small head

Dark brown or grey-brown back

Grey or grey-brown dorsal fin is set well back on body with 9 rays

Small scales covered in slime. Scale count: 49–60

Light brown or bronze sides

Yellow, cream or buff belly

Long-based, grey or grey-brown anal fin with 23–31 branched rays

Pale grey pectoral and pelvic fins with darker tips

Low mouth extends like bellows into a feeding tube

Small eyes with diameter less than or same as length of snout

c 25–50cm

Pharyngeal teeth: 5 : 5

Distribution
Widespread throughout much of Europe from France and Britain eastwards, the bream is mainly a fish of lowland eutrophic lakes, canals, fenland drains and the lower reaches of big rivers. Bream have been introduced to Ireland.

The bream is a very deep-bodied fish with moderately flattened sides and a high back, which is especially noticeable in larger specimens. It has a small head and a low mouth. Its eyes are relatively small – their diameter is less than the length of the snout in larger bream and never greater than the length of the snout in smaller bream. The scales are small and covered with copious slime. In the breeding season males develop many white or yellowish tubercles on the head and shoulders.

Younger, smaller bream are predominantly silver with dark grey-brown backs. These can easily be confused with other bream species (see below). Older, larger bream have a dark brown or grey-brown back shading to lighter brown or bronze on the sides and yellow, cream or buff on the belly. The fins are grey or grey-brown. In some northern, clear-water lakes large bream may retain part of their juvenile coloration with a steel-grey back, dull silver sides and a white belly.

Bream can be easily confused with Danube bream (see pages 108–9), blue bream (see pages 106–7) and silver bream (see pages 110–11). Check for eye diameter, sliminess, scale counts, anal fin rays, the relative positions of the front of anal fin base and rear of dorsal fin base, pharyngeal teeth and fin colour. All these features are diagnostic.

Breeding behaviour and life cycle

Bream that have overwintered in brackish lagoons or close to a river estuary migrate upstream in late April to May to spawn in freshwater. Males obtain territories in areas of shallow water, often in weedy areas and spawning occurs from May to July when the water temperature has reached 12°C. In some northern lakes breeding may not occur every year because the water will not become warm enough.

Tiny, 1.5mm-diameter, yellow eggs are laid at night on weeds or clear gravel where they stick. They are laid in batches, often at intervals of three to six days over a three to four week period, each female producing an equivalent of 80,000–110,000 eggs per kilogram of body weight.

Hatching occurs three to 14 days after fertilization and the 4–5mm-long larval bream remain attached to their natal weed or gravel until their yolk sacs are completely absorbed. They then stay in the shallow water until winter, feeding on algae and planktonic organisms. After spawning, adults return immediately to deeper water.

Food and feeding behaviour

The bream is primarily a bottom-feeding shoal fish, grubbing about in mud and silt for food such as insect larvae, snails, small bivalve molluscs and worms. Clouds of mud often betray the presence of feeding bream shoals. There are also many records of large bream feeding in mid-water on small fish fry in summer. Juvenile bream frequently feed close to the surface on hatching midges in summer and these actions gave rise to their nickname 'skimmers'.

Growth and longevity

Some ponds have large populations of stunted bream, where maturity is reached after eight to 10 years when the fish have reached 20–25cm in length. Similar slow growth rates and delayed maturity also occurs in lakes at the northern limit of the bream's range. By contrast, growth is much more rapid in larger, eutrophic waters. Here bream will grow to 5–8cm after one year; 8–13cm after two years; 12–16cm after three years; 15–20cm after four years; and 18–25cm after five years. The fish mature here in their fourth or fifth year. After 10 years, such fish can be 50–60cm long and weigh 2.5–3kg. Bream may live for 20 years or more with exceptional lengths of over 80cm and weights of 9kg or more.

Predators

The bream is a favourite prey species of the pike and in Low Country canals, reedy meres and Irish loughs this species is preferred to the equally abundant roach. Bream fry are also important prey for large rainbow trout in lowland reservoirs. The only fish-eating bird that can cope with a medium-sized bream is the cormorant, although gulls and occasionally common terns will hunt shoals of bream fry in lake margins.

Conservation status of bream
This species is often abundant, usually occurring in large shoals of mixed sizes and ages throughout its range.

Danube Bream *Abramis sapa*

Of all four European bream species, this is perhaps the least well-known, providing identification problems for the visiting angler or naturalist.

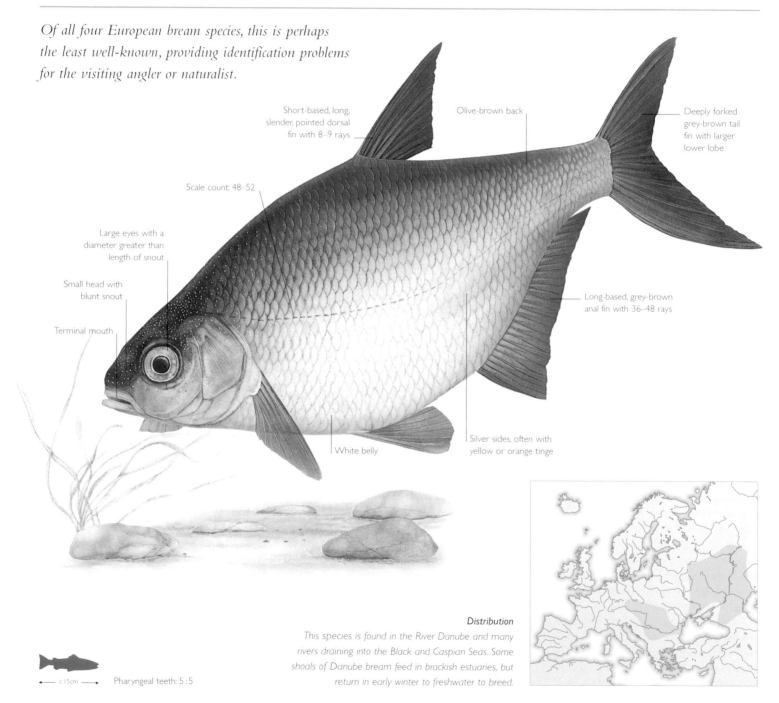

Short-based, long, slender, pointed dorsal fin with 8–9 rays

Olive-brown back

Deeply forked grey-brown tail fin with larger lower lobe

Scale count: 48–52

Large eyes with a diameter greater than length of snout

Small head with blunt snout

Terminal mouth

Long-based, grey-brown anal fin with 36–48 rays

White belly

Silver sides, often with yellow or orange tinge

c.15cm

Pharyngeal teeth: 5 : 5

Distribution
This species is found in the River Danube and many rivers draining into the Black and Caspian Seas. Some shoals of Danube bream feed in brackish estuaries, but return in early winter to freshwater to breed.

The Danube bream is the smallest bream and any bream longer than 20cm is likely to be another species. It has a moderately deep body (in adults not as deep as the bronze bream) that is extremely laterally flattened. The head is small, the snout blunt and the mouth terminal. The eyes are much larger than the very similar blue bream's (eye diameter is greater than the length of the snout, whereas the blue bream's eye diameter equals snout length).

Another useful pointer is the tail fin, which is deeply forked and has a larger lower than upper lobe (the blue bream's lobes are equal in size). The anal fin is extremely long-based and the dorsal fin short-based, but this is long, slender and pointed.

The coloration of the Danube bream's back is usually olive-brown, but is grey-green in clear waters. The sides are silver, often with a yellow or olive tinge, and the belly is white. The fins are all grey-brown with lighter rays. Spawning males have many whitish tubercles on the head, front half of the body and pectoral and pelvic fins.

For other differences between this and other bream species see page 105.

Breeding behaviour and life cycle

As water temperatures begin to rise from the winter low during the months of March or April, Danube bream begin their migration upstream from deep lowland pools and brackish estuarine reaches to their spawning areas of gravel-bottomed, streamy runs in the main river, which contain dense weed beds. They do not pair, but remain in small shoals so when a female sheds her eggs the chances of successful fertilisation are enhanced by several males simultaneously releasing milt.

The 1.5mm-diameter yellow eggs are laid between mid-April and the end of May over weed. Each female produces 40,000–50,000 eggs: one large 24cm-long female produced about 48,000, while a 19cm fish yielded about 38,500.

After spawning is over, adults move swiftly downstream to their feeding areas. The eggs hatch after five to 10 days, and the 4–5mm-long larvae remain in the weeds for up to four days, until their yolk sacs are completely exhausted. They then seek microscopic food (unicellular algae, tiny crustaceans) within the weed beds until they have grown to approximately 2cm. The fry then turn to the smaller items in the adult diet, but remain close to their spawning areas until the autumn when they start to migrate downstream to reach deeper pools.

Food and feeding behaviour

The Danube bream is primarily a bottom-feeding shoal fish, taking whatever is available that it can ingest. In the lower river reaches, this includes midge larvae, crustaceans and molluscs including snails and pea-mussels. Those that penetrate brackish water feed mainly on gammarid crustaceans and small bivalve molluscs.

Growth and longevity

The Danube bream is a small fish, reaching 4–5cm after one year, 8–10cm after two years, 12–15 cm after three years and 15–20cm after four years. Exceptionally large specimens may grow to 25–30cm and weigh over 750g. It matures at three to four years and rarely lives for more than five or six years.

Predators

Nobody knows for certain which animals eat Danube bream, but predators probably include piscivorous fish such as pike, perch and zander and fish-eating birds, such as kingfishers, herons and white pelicans.

Shoal behaviour or a solitary existence

It is a fact that most freshwater fish that do not eat other fish live in shoals, whereas most freshwater fish that do eat other fish are solitary hunters. It is also noticeable that the smaller fish of some species (for example, ide pages 82–83 and asp pages 118–19) are shoal fish, but that they tend to become solitary as they grow into fish-eaters.

The reason why, in rivers and lakes, it pays predators to be solitary is obvious. It is easier to sneak up on a prey species when alone; if there are two predators trying to get near a potential prey the chances of being seen are doubled.

Furthermore, when one of the predators moves to catch its food, the shoal of forage-fish will flee, leaving the other predator without food.

However it is not so obvious why there is an advantage in forage-fish, or potential prey such as the various species of bream, roach and bleak, living in shoals. The argument used to be that there was 'safety in numbers'; that many pairs of eyes might notice the approaching predator and warn the entire shoals so that they might flee together (see Raising the alarm on page 101). The fact that we see the shoal flee when a potential predator approaches suggests that the 'safety in numbers' argument works to foil predators. Yet the fact that predators manage to catch enough from the shoals to survive suggests that it is not so simple.

When a solitary predator catches prey from amongst a shoal, the likelihood is that weak, injured or diseased shoal members are going to be caught first. Observations on perch and small pike, hunting bream and roach fry and large trout stalking minnows are amongst many that confirm this. The result is that, by the predator selecting the weak, the shoal is improved. It is an example of survival of the fittest by natural selection.

It is interesting, in this respect, that some larger predators (for example, the pike and zander) are solitary hunters but shoal fish when not hunting. And that fish that are shoal fish when feeding on tiny particles (for example, perch on midge pupae) become solitary when hunting bream fry in lake shallows.

Conservation status of Danube bream
This bream has declined during the last 50 years in many of its native rivers. Damming is a major problem in some rivers, including the Danube itself, as it prevents adults moving upstream to their shallow, weedy spawning areas. Pollution has also resulted in declines in other rivers, especially where the lower reaches traditionally used by feeding Danube bream have been affected. This species is now close to being endangered and its populations need careful, regular monitoring.

Zahrte *Vimba vimba*

This eastern European fish is one of the most colourful members of the carp family; it is also one of the most migratory, travelling up to 500km within the river systems where it is found.

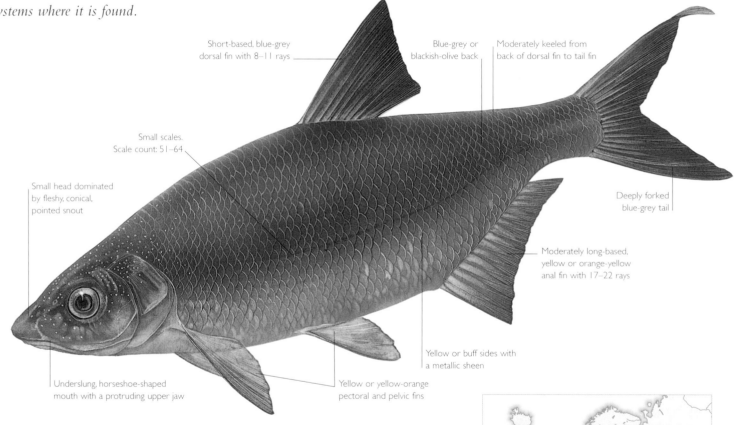

Short-based, blue-grey dorsal fin with 8–11 rays

Blue-grey or blackish-olive back

Moderately keeled from back of dorsal fin to tail fin

Small scales. Scale count: 51–64

Small head dominated by fleshy, conical, pointed snout

Deeply forked blue-grey tail

Moderately long-based, yellow or orange-yellow anal fin with 17–22 rays

Underslung, horseshoe-shaped mouth with a protruding upper jaw

Yellow or yellow-orange pectoral and pelvic fins

Yellow or buff sides with a metallic sheen

c.25cm

Pharyngeal teeth: 5:5

Distribution

This eastern European fish is recorded from the lowest river reaches in northern Germany and southern Sweden, Poland and the Baltic States eastwards and southwards to the Black and Caspian Seas. It is also found in Baltic lagoons and lowland lakes set on large river systems.

The zahrte is a fairly slender fish with slightly flattened sides. The back is moderately ridged or keeled from the rear of the dorsal fin to the tail fin base, and the underside is keeled between the pelvic and anal fins. The latter keel is scaleless. It has a small head dominated by a fleshy, conical, pointed snout, which is longer than the diameter of the eye.

Adapted for feeding on the river bottom, the mouth is conspicuously underslung and horseshoe-shaped; the upper jaw protrudes well beyond the lower. The scales are very small compared with many in the carp family. The dorsal fin is very short-based, the anal fin moderately long-based and the tail fin is deeply forked.

Outside of the breeding season the coloration is somewhat subdued, with a blue-grey or blackish-olive back, yellow or buff sides with a metallic sheen and a paler belly. Both sexes develop spawning tubercles and a mating coloration in the breeding season. The males' upper parts become very dark, sooty grey, sometimes blue-black, and the jaws, throat and belly from around the base of the pectoral fins to the bottom edge of the tail fin develop into a bright orange-red. The dorsal and tail fins darken from blue-grey to almost jet black, and the pectoral, pelvic and anal fins turn from yellow or orange-yellow to bright orange.

Females usually develop a subdued version of the male spawning dress, but some retain a drabber grey and buff coloration.

Breeding behaviour and life cycle
The zahrte migrates up to and over 500km within its natal river systems, feeding as far downstream as the brackish estuary and swimming upstream to spawn. Damming has reduced these migrations in many rivers and endangered many populations (see Conservation status box). From March to June the fish move upstream to their spawning areas – shallow, weedy, gravel-bottomed reaches of the main river or small tributaries.

Mating appears to take place mainly at night. More than one male may fertilise one female's eggs and most females shed their eggs in batches over several evenings. Such a promiscuous

spawning system is commonly found in cyprinids and has several advantages over a monogamous system. By mating with several males, the female almost guarantees 100 per cent fertilisation of her eggs. And by having several males fertilise her egges, her progeny have greater genetic variability than if her eggs were fertilised by one male.

Each female produces approximately 100,000–200,000, 1.5mm-diameter, creamy yellow eggs over loose gravel, which either stick to pebbles or are washed into cavities. They hatch after about five to 10 days and the 6mm-long larvae rest on the bottom until their yolk sacs are absorbed (they do not remain stuck to rocks as do most carp larvae). The larvae then start feeding on tiny algae and invertebrates and remain in the spawning area until the autumn. Adult zahrte migrate downstream immediately after spawning, feeding as they go.

Food and feeding behaviour
The zahrte is a shoaling bottom-feeder, taking insect larvae, especially midge larvae, small molluscs, such as snails and pea-mussels, and annelid and tubificid worms from muddy or silty substrates. Those that move as far downstream as brackish water also take small crustaceans, mainly gammarids, and polychaete worms.

Zahrte grub their food from the river bottom and detect food with the sensitive nerve endings in their fleshy lips. Feeding activity slows down greatly when water temperatures fall below about 6°C in winter.

Growth and longevity
Growth is slow: zahrte are approximately 10–12cm after two to four years, 20cm after five to seven years, and 30cm or more, weighing 450–500g, after eight to 10 years. Zahrte exceptionally grow to 50cm long and reach 0.9–1kg in weight. Most mature at four years and few live for more than 10 years.

Predators
Birds and fish, including herons, cormorants, white pelicans and pike, are the major predators. Fry are vulnerable to kingfishers, asp, perch and zander.

The zahrte is one of the few small- to medium-sized members of the carp family to have been commercially fished.

Mating dress and spawning tubercles
In many cyprinids the coloration of the males brightens just before the onset of the spawning season – the zahrte is a good example of this. The more brightly coloured a male fish, the greater chance that a female will choose him to fertilise at least some of her eggs. Besides attracting the females, the gaudy mating dress of many fish is also used as a signal to warn off other males who might try to compete for the attention of the females. In three-spined sticklebacks, for instance, males will attack other males as soon as they see their bright red throat (see pages 156–57). They will also attack any other red object that invades their territory, such as an angler's red fly or spinner or a piece of red Plasticine suspended by a thread!

However, the function of spawning or nuptial tubercles is not fully understood. These tiny white or cream pimple-like structures develop as spawning approaches and disappear after spawning. In some species, such as the dace, they develop only in the males, but in others, such as the zahrte, both sexes have them. Incidentally, some anglers have caught fish with tubercles and, thinking that they have some sort of disease, destroyed the fish in order 'to prevent others being infected'!

Conservation status of zahrte
In many rivers the zahrte population has declined because shoals cannot travel as far and exploit great lengths of river as they once did. Damming has provided an impassable physical barrier and pollution a chemical barrier, although the zahrte does appear to be able to tolerate a degree of organic pollution. It is now a rare and endangered fish in Germany, Poland and Sweden and needs protection. It is, however, reported to be thriving in rivers draining into the Black and Caspian Seas.

Danube Bleak *Chalcalburnus chalcoides*

This small, silvery fish has a scattered distribution in the Danube catchment area and, although it is numerous, not much is known about it.

The Danube bleak is a very slender fish and its laterally flattened body is covered with tiny scales that are difficult to detach. Males develop tiny tubercles on the head and shoulders in the breeding season.

Breeding behaviour and life cycle
Danube bleak spawn from late April to June. Spawning occurs in shallow stream riffles with fine gravel-bottoms or gravel fans at feeder stream mouths. These are communal spawners – each female is pursued by up to five males. Each female produces about 30,000, 1.5mm-diameter, pale yellow eggs, which fall into cavities and stick within the gravel. The 3–4mm-long larvae hatch after about two weeks. After spawning the adults return to their feeding areas.

Food and feeding behaviour
Danube bleak are mid-water to surface shoal fish. Lake and brackish water populations probably take much of their food by filter-feeding zooplankton.

All Danube bleak also eat large amounts of midge pupae rising to hatch at the water surface and adult insects on the surface. In winter, when these foods are scarce, some foods, such worms and snails, are taken from the river or lake bed.

Growth and longevity
Most Danube bleak grow to 15–20cm, some reaching 25cm. Lengths of 30cm are exceptional, but some Black Sea populations are reported at 40cm. They rarely live for more than five years, but these points need further research.

Predators
This species is a potentially important food source for fish-eating birds in the Black Sea and estuaries, such as pelicans, and for fish, such as zander.

Distribution and habitat
The two main populations are one in Austrian alpine lakes and one in the lower Danube and rivers flowing into the Black, Aral and Caspian Seas.

Conservation status of Danube bleak
This species is common in slower river reaches and in some alpine lakes throughout its range. However, populations that feed in brackish water are at risk from river damming in the lower reaches, which may prevent them migrating to their freshwater spawning areas.

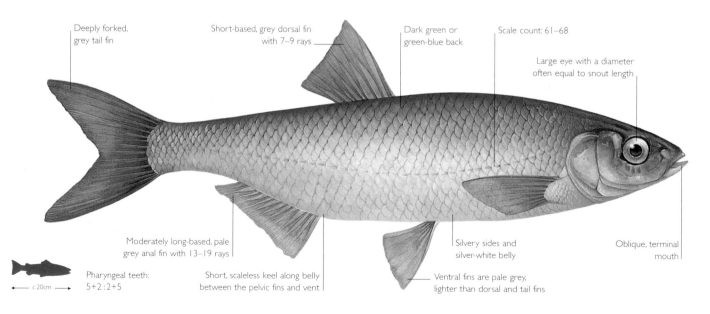

Deeply forked, grey tail fin

Short-based, grey dorsal fin with 7–9 rays

Dark green or green-blue back

Scale count: 61–68

Large eye with a diameter often equal to snout length

Moderately long-based, pale grey anal fin with 13–19 rays

Pharyngeal teeth: 5+2 : 2+5

c 20cm

Short, scaleless keel along belly between the pelvic fins and vent

Silvery sides and silver-white belly

Ventral fins are pale grey, lighter than dorsal and tail fins

Oblique, terminal mouth

Schneider *Alburnoides bipunctatus*

This distinctive little fish is a characteristic species of small, clear, mainland European trout streams and it occasionally occurs in cool lakes.

This is a small shoal fish with a deeper body than the bleak. Its body is covered with tiny, secure scales except for a short, scaleless keel between the pelvic fins and vent. Males develop tiny white tubercles on the head during the breeding season.

Breeding behaviour and life cycle
Schneider spawn in May to June in shallow river reaches where well-oxygenated, streamy water flows over coarse sand or gravel. It is probably a communal breeder, the eggs from each female being fertilised by sperm from several males. Females probably lay less than 10,000 eggs per fish. Nothing is known about the incubation period, but the 1.5mm-diameter, yellow eggs probably hatch after about 10 days.

Food and feeding behaviour
The schneider appears to be more of a bottom-feeder than the bleak. Shoals often congregate on the bottom of fast riffles. They will rise to take insects hatching at the surface of the water, and land-bred insects that have fallen onto the water. In winter feeding intensity declines as they seek deep water.

Growth and longevity
Again, little is known, but the schneider usually grows to a maximum length of 10–12cm, exceptionally 15cm. It probably first spawns in its second year and rarely lives for more than five years, but these points need further research.

Predators
Fish, including large brown trout, small pike, chub, asp and perch, are probably the main predators.

Distribution and habitat
Schneider occur in fast-flowing rivers and clean lakes from France eastwards through Germany, the Low Countries and central Europe to Russia, but is absent from Iberia, Iceland, Fenno-Scandinavia, the British Isles, the Baltic states, northern Russia, Italy, Greece and the Alpine regions.

Conservation status of schneider
The schneider is common and sometimes abundant throughout its range.

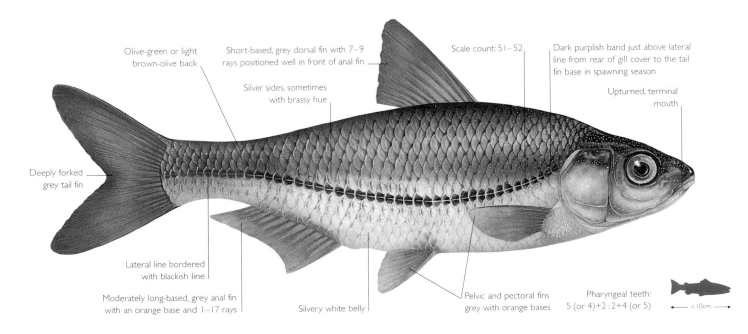

Olive-green or light brown-olive back

Short-based, grey dorsal fin with 7–9 rays positioned well in front of anal fin

Scale count: 51–52

Dark purplish band just above lateral line from rear of gill cover to the tail fin base in spawning season

Silver sides, sometimes with brassy hue

Upturned, terminal mouth

Deeply forked grey tail fin

Lateral line bordered with blackish line

Moderately long-based, grey anal fin with an orange base and 1–17 rays

Silvery white belly

Pelvic and pectoral fins grey with orange bases

Pharyngeal teeth: 5 (or 4)+2 : 2+4 (or 5)

c.10cm

Thracian Barbel *Barbus cyclolepis*

This barbel is representative of those found only in southeastern Europe. Other closely related barbel may be better ascribed to this species and not considered species in their own right.

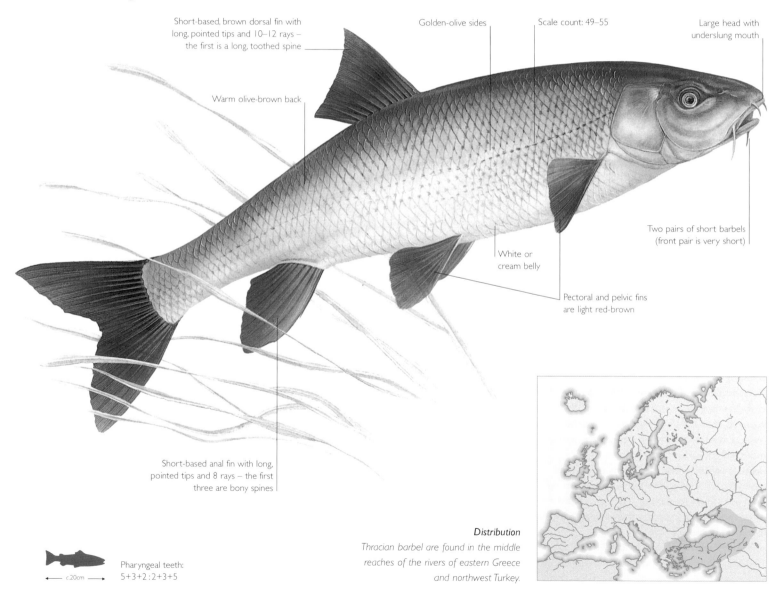

Short-based, brown dorsal fin with long, pointed tips and 10–12 rays – the first is a long, toothed spine

Warm olive-brown back

Golden-olive sides

Scale count: 49–55

Large head with underslung mouth

Two pairs of short barbels (front pair is very short)

White or cream belly

Pectoral and pelvic fins are light red-brown

Short-based anal fin with long, pointed tips and 8 rays – the first three are bony spines

c.20cm

Pharyngeal teeth: 5+3+2:2+3+5

Distribution
Thracian barbel are found in the middle reaches of the rivers of eastern Greece and northwest Turkey.

This small barbel has a long, slender build, but is round in cross section and not as flattened underneath as the other barbel species. Its large head has an underslung mouth with thick lips and two pairs of short barbels; the front pair is very short (less than half the length of the second pair) and the second pair are equal in length to the eye diameter, which is shorter than in other barbel species. The dorsal and anal fins are short-based, fairly long and pointed at the tips.

The back is a warm olive-brown, the sides are golden-olive and the belly is white or cream. The fins are brown, but the pectoral, pelvic and anal fins are a lighter red-brown. The males develop white or cream tubercles on their head and shoulders at the onset of the breeding season.

Breeding behaviour and life cycle

Adult Thracian barbels move to the nearest suitable gravel-bottomed, fast-flowing, shallow riffle (about 40cm deep) during late March to early May. Here several males may joust for the attention of one ripe female, chasing her around and barging into each other if they manage to swim alongside her. Eventually she releases her eggs and this triggers males close by to shed milt to fertilise the eggs. After spawning the adults return immediately to their feeding areas.

Each female produces 6000–12,000 yellow, 2mm-diameter, heavy eggs, which sink into the gravel. The 5–6mm-long larvae hatch after about eight days at water temperatures of 15–17°C. About three days later, when their yolk sacs are completely exhausted, the fry swim from the gravel spawning areas to the shallow river margins where they feed on algae and microscopic invertebrates. They eventually swim to deeper water in autumn and begin to eat adult foods.

Food and feeding behaviour

The Thracian barbel finds most of its food in the river bed, using its sensitive barbels and lips to identify potential food. Midge and caddis larvae, mayfly and stonefly nymphs, aquatic snails, freshwater shrimps and worms all feature in the diet. They also eat algae and can sometimes be seen grazing algae from boulders or bridge piers.

In summer, peak feeding activity appears to occur from dusk into the night. Feeding activity reduces as water temperatures fall in late autumn and the fish often hibernate under fallen tree trunks, branches or rafts of flood debris in the cold months of January and February.

Growth and longevity

Thracian barbel are relatively small, growing to only 5–6cm after one year, 10–12cm after two years, about 15cm after three years and 20cm after four years, when they mature. Maximum length is usually about 25cm and weight about 500g. Exceptionally specimens may reach lengths of more than 30cm and weights over 1kg.

Predators

Nobody knows for sure which animals predate this fish, but some fry are probably taken by kingfishers, chub and trout, while herons and cormorants might occasionally feed on adults.

Further research

Taxonomically the barbels are a complicated group of fish. Here a simple arrangement has been suggested: three main species (barbel, Mediterranean barbel, Thracian barbel) with six other species (Iberian, Portuguese, Italian, Peloponnesian, Euboean and Greek barbels) that are closely related to the three main species.

However, further research may indicate that this simple approach requires modification. For example the three species descibed here from the Iberian Peninsula (the Iberian *Barbus bocagei*, the Portuguese *B. comiza* and the most westerly population of the Mediterranean barbel *B. mendionalis*) have been split into seven species by some researchers and named as follows: *B. bocagei, B. comiza, B. graellsii, B. guiraonis, B. haasi, B. microcephalus* and *B. scalteri*.

Similarly in southeast Europe, from Italy eastwards, the barbel overlaps with the Mediterranean barbel, which overlaps with the Thracian barbel and four other speices have been described that might be subspecies of one of the these: *B. plebejus*, a subspecies of *B. barbus, B. pelopennesius* of *B. meridionalis, B. euboicus* and

B. graecus of *B. cyclolepis*. Yet there is also the question as to whether the Mediterranean barbel has other valid subspecies: *B. m. caninus* from the rivers draining the Italian Alps and the *B. m. petenyi* from the Danube system. The entire situation is in need of urgent, objective research including thorough DNA analyses of all European barbel populations.

White-finned Gudgeon *Gobio albipinnatus*

This southeast European gudgeon has been neglected by naturalists because of its small size, economic unimportance and fairly restricted distribution.

This is a small fish with a rounded, sturdy body that tapers to a slender tail. Its throat is scaleless. The large head has a ventral mouth with fleshy lips bearing one barbel at each corner of the mouth. The white-finned gudgeon's barbels are much longer than the gudgeon's and are two to three times the eye diameter.

The high dorsal fin is short-based and positioned above the pelvic fins; the anal fin is short-based; and the tail fin is large and forked. The male has tiny tubercles on his head and shoulders during the spawning season.

Breeding behaviour and life cycle

Little is known about the white-finned gudgeon's life cycle, but it certainly spawns in late April to June, probably at night, over weed to which its 1.5mm-diameter, blue-grey eggs stick. The eggs are probably laid in batches over several days. Nine females held an average 1860 eggs (ranging from 1250 to 2970). The young remain in shallow water until winter.

Food and feeding behaviour

The white-finned gudgeon is a bottom-feeder and midge larvae and pupae dominate the diet (13 out of 19 specimens had only these in their stomachs, while the other six contained midge larvae and tiny annelid worms).

Growth and longevity

This species grows to a maximum length of 10–12cm. Females are longer than males of the same age. Life expectancy is about five years.

Predators

Larger fish, including chub, perch and zander, and birds such as grey herons and kingfishers are likely to take large numbers of white-finned gudgeon.

Distribution and habitat

A species of the slow-flowing, usually silt- or mud-bottomed rivers, this fish occur in the lower reaches of the Danube and other rivers flowing into the Black and Caspian Seas.

Conservation status of white-finned gudgeon
This is a common species, but it is easily overlooked because of its habits of feeding on the bottom of rivers.

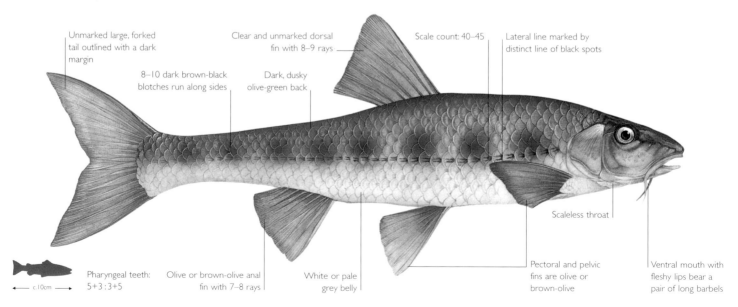

Unmarked large, forked tail outlined with a dark margin

Clear and unmarked dorsal fin with 8–9 rays

Scale count: 40–45

Lateral line marked by distinct line of black spots

8–10 dark brown-black blotches run along sides

Dark, dusky olive-green back

Scaleless throat

Pharyngeal teeth: 5+3:3+5

Olive or brown-olive anal fin with 7–8 rays

White or pale grey belly

Pectoral and pelvic fins are olive or brown-olive

Ventral mouth with fleshy lips bear a pair of long barbels

c.10cm

Kessler's Gudgeon *Gobio kessleri*

This scarce species of gudgeon, which lives in fast-flowing streams of two central European rivers, has been little studied.

Conservation status of Kessler's gudgeon
This species has become relatively rare due, on the whole, to the proliferation of dams on its rivers. It should now be considered as an endangered species.

This is a long, slender gudgeon, with a generally rounded body and a slightly flattened belly between the pelvic fins. It has a large head, a wide, ventral mouth, fleshy lips and a barbel at each corner of the mouth (the barbel length is two to three times eye diameter). The dorsal fin is fairly long, the anal fin shorter and the forked tail fin is at the end of a very thin, rounded tail. The underside of the body is scaleless.

Breeding behaviour and life cycle
So little is known about Kessler's gudgeon that its breeding behaviour is virtually unknown. It is probably similar to the gudgeon's. In two Austrian streams, spawning occurs in May or June among gravel in shallow water (less than 50cm deep) close to the bank. The eggs are sticky, about 1.5mm in diameter, and are a drab grey-buff. One 7cm female carried about 1100 eggs. Hatching occurs after about three weeks and the fry probably spend their first few months feeding in the spawning shallows.

Food and feeding behaviour
The Kessler's gudgeon is a bottom-feeder and it probably eats any small invertebrates it can find in the boulder/gravel river bed. Its food probably includes tiny stonefly and mayfly nymphs, midge and blackfly larvae, microcaddis larvae, crustaceans and small snails.

Growth and longevity
Seven specimens averaged approximately 8cm (but can range from 6 to 11cm) and the maximum length reported is 12cm. This species probably lives for about five years.

Predators
Large brown trout and chub are probably the greatest predators of the Kessler's gudgeon.

Distribution and habitat
This is a species of fast-flowing reaches and tributaries of the upper and middle Danube and Dnestr river systems.

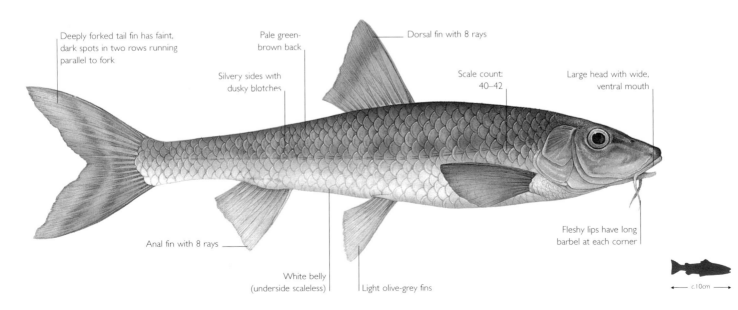

Deeply forked tail fin has faint, dark spots in two rows running parallel to fork

Pale green-brown back

Dorsal fin with 8 rays

Silvery sides with dusky blotches

Scale count: 40–42

Large head with wide, ventral mouth

Anal fin with 8 rays

White belly (underside scaleless)

Light olive-grey fins

Fleshy lips have long barbel at each corner

c.10cm

Tench *Tinca tinca*

Although many people have heard of the tench, relatively few non-anglers will have seen one. They live on the bottom of weedy meres in water that is usually too murky to see through.

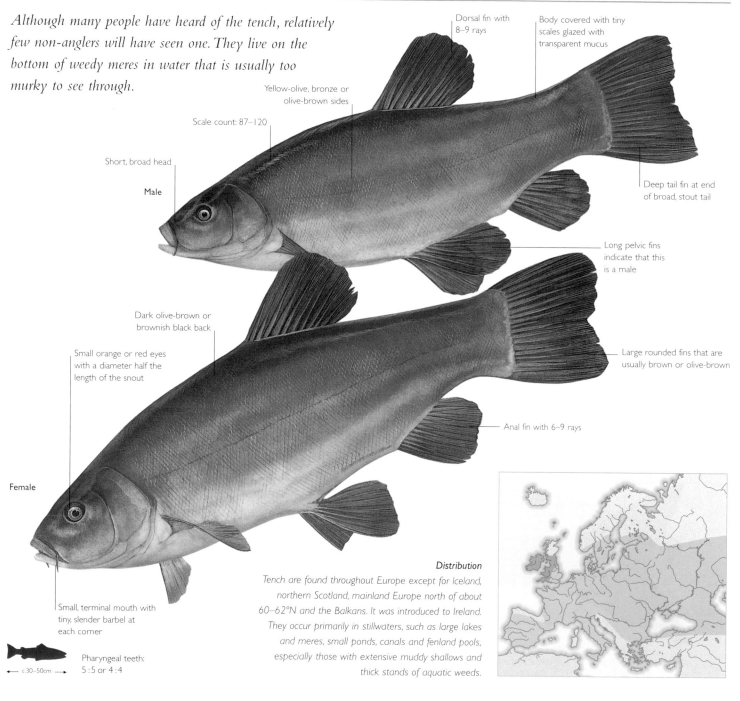

Dorsal fin with 8–9 rays

Body covered with tiny scales glazed with transparent mucus

Yellow-olive, bronze or olive-brown sides

Scale count: 87–120

Short, broad head

Male

Deep tail fin at end of broad, stout tail

Long pelvic fins indicate that this is a male

Dark olive-brown or brownish black back

Small orange or red eyes with a diameter half the length of the snout

Large rounded fins that are usually brown or olive-brown

Anal fin with 6–9 rays

Female

Small, terminal mouth with tiny, slender barbel at each corner

c.30–50cm

Pharyngeal teeth: 5:5 or 4:4

Distribution

Tench are found throughout Europe except for Iceland, northern Scotland, mainland Europe north of about 60–62°N and the Balkans. It was introduced to Ireland. They occur primarily in stillwaters, such as large lakes and meres, small ponds, canals and fenland pools, especially those with extensive muddy shallows and thick stands of aquatic weeds.

The tench is a summer fish: from autumn to late spring it hibernates on lake beds.

The tench's body is sturdy, thickset and laterally flattened, especially along the tail. It is covered with tiny, inconspicuous scales that are glazed with thick, transparent mucus. The head is short, but broad, and its mouth is small and terminal with a tiny, slender barbel at each corner. The eyes are small with a diameter about half the snout length. All fins are large and rounded: the tail fin is deep at the end of the broad, stout tail; the anal and dorsal fins are relatively short-based; and the pelvic fins are long.

After the second year, when he is at least 12–15cm long, the male's second pelvic fin ray, which is the first full-length ray, is thick and fleshy, and the pelvic fins extend to or beyond the vent. The female's second ray is not thick and fleshy, and her pelvic fins are shorter.

Coloration is variable. Most tench are very dark olive-brown or brownish-black on the back, yellow-olive, bronze or olive-brown on the sides, and yellow, olive or whitish on the belly. The fins are usually dark brown or olive-brown, although some tench have orange-red fins. The eyes are orange or red. There is also a golden form of tench, where the body is golden-orange with irregular, dark spotting, and there is a very rare vermilion form with an olive back, greenish sides and deep vermilion belly. These forms probably originate from released ornamental stocks.

Breeding behaviour and life cycle

Spawning occurs only when the water temperature reaches at least 19–20°C. This will be in May in southern Europe, but in the north of its range, it may be as late as July. In cold springs tench may fail to breed in northern lakes.

Weedy shallows are chosen for spawning and ripe females are pursued by several males into dense weeds. This chase triggers a female into releasing a batch of 1–1.5mm-diameter, green eggs, which are fertilised by milt shed by the males and then stick to the weed. Each female lays her total egg mass (which is equivalent to 100,000–150,000 per kilogram of her body weight) in batches over several days.

The 4–5mm larval tench hatch in three to eight days, depending on the temperature, and cling to their natal weed bed for seven to 10 days until their yolk sacs have been fully absorbed. They then slowly disperse and begin to feed actively on zooplankton among the relative security of the weed bed.

Food and feeding behaviour

Tench fry eat zooplankton, especially rotifers and crustaceans, such as cladocerans, ostracods and copepods. As they grow, they turn increasingly to the adult diet of insect larvae, especially midge larvae, worms and water hog-lice. They also eat some aquatic plant material including algae and pondweed leaves. As tench root about on the bottom, with snouts down and tails up, lots of tiny air bubbles, some no bigger than a pin head, float to the surface, betraying the presence of shoals.

Tench are almost exclusively warm weather feeders and feeding intensity falls as the water temperature dips below 15°C. The fish cease feeding and hibernate on the bottom in deep water when the water temperature falls below 10–12°C. They can tolerate quite high water temperatures, certainly over 30°C, but in bright, hot summer weather they tend to become crepuscular feeders.

Growth and longevity

In its first year a tench fry will grow from 4–5mm to 8cm, weighing about 10g; up to 15cm and 100g after two years; and up to 30cm and 300g after three years. Most spawn for the first time at three years old. Growth depends largely on water productivity and the length of time the water temperature remains around 15°C each year. In some lakes three-year-old tench have been recorded weighing 800g; in small, overstocked ponds they will average less than 150g. Maximum length is usually about 50cm, weighing about 2kg, but in very productive waters they may reach 70cm and 8kg, and live for 10 to 15 years.

Predators

Tench fry are eaten by fish, such as pike and perch. In one weedy lowland lake stocked with rainbow trout, many of the trout hunted tench fry in the weedy margins during late July and August.

Conservation status of tench
Common and often abundant, the tench is carefully protected by anglers who admire this striking fish.

Identifying Cyprinid Hybrids

Because most cyprinids spawn in shoals and sperm is shed by many males, sometimes over a fairly wide area, whenever a female sheds her eggs, there is always the possibility that sperm from one species will inadvertently fertilise the eggs of another species spawning nearby. The consequence of cross-fertilisation is a hybrid offspring and this can be confused with one of the parent species.

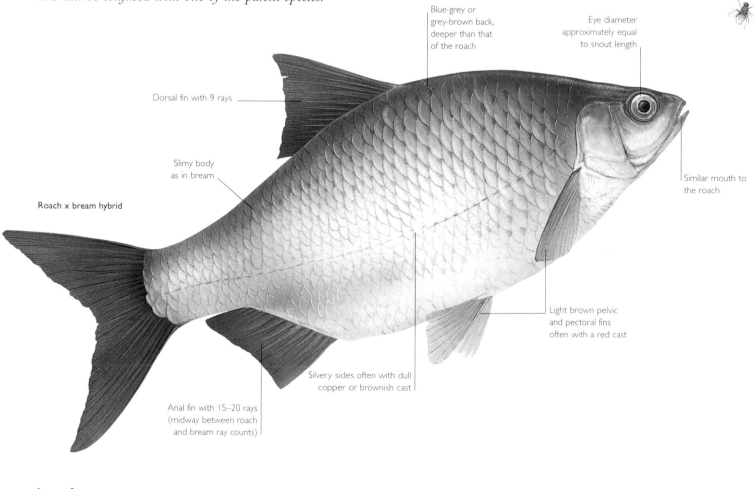

Blue-grey or grey-brown back, deeper than that of the roach

Eye diameter approximately equal to snout length

Dorsal fin with 9 rays

Slimy body as in bream

Roach x bream hybrid

Similar mouth to the roach

Light brown pelvic and pectoral fins often with a red cast

Silvery sides often with dull copper or brownish cast

Anal fin with 15–20 rays (midway between roach and bream ray counts)

c.25–30cm

Most hybrids are sterile, but there are two main exceptions to this rule, namely the roach x bream and the roach x rudd. These two hybrids are often found in Ireland and a proportion of them have been reported to be fertile. Hybridisation appears to be commonest in waters in which the parent species have recently been introduced. This is true of the roach, rudd and bream, which have been introduced in Ireland. Hybridisation in cyprinids does not come about as the result of mating between the parent species. Cyprinids often mate communally, with vast numbers of sperm and eggs being shed simultaneously in shallow water. If two different species are spawning on the same shallow area, then eggs of one may inadvertently be fertilised by the sperm from another, resulting in the hybrid.

Hybrids usually display some characteristics from each of the parent species, although they may more closely resemble one of them. The following list describes the commoner hybrids found in Europe.

Roach x bream

This is a very common hybrid. It resembles a very deep-bodied roach with a dull sheen on its sides. It has a roach's mouth, but is usually slimy like a bream. The number of branched rays in the anal fin (15–20) will confirm that it is a hybrid.

Roach x bleak

This hybrid is deeper bodied than the bleak and it has orange pelvic and anal fins. Its mouth is level as in the roach. Once again, the number of branched rays in the anal fin (13–15) will confirm that it is a hybrid. Its pharyngeal teeth are also diagnostic: 5 (or 6)+1 (or 2) : 1 (or 2)+5 (or 6) (smooth or very slightly serrated and with a slight hook at the tip).

Roach x silver bream

A deep-bodied, silvery looking fish with orange pelvic and anal fins, this hybrid also has an orange or yellow iris (red in roach and grey in silver bream). Its eye is proportionally smaller than the silver bream's. The number of branched rays in its anal fin (16–18) will confirm identification.

Roach x rudd

The roach x rudd is an extremely common hybrid. Identification can be certain only when several external factors are taken into account and/or the fish is killed and its pharyngeal teeth thoroughly examined.
- The front of the dorsal fin base lies behind the pelvic fin base, but not as far behind as that of the rudd.
- The hybrid's lips are level and its mouth resembles the roach's.
- There is usually a keel on the belly (similar to the rudd).
- General coloration tends to resemble that of the rudd, but the roach x rudd has orange fins and an orange iris.
- Pharyngeal teeth: 5 (or 6)+1 (or 2) : 1 (or 2)+5 (or 6) – moderately serrated. Note that the tiny 1 or 2 teeth in the second row are often broken, but their bases can usually be distinguished.

Carp x crucian carp

Similar in shape to the crucian, this hybrid has thinner and shorter version of the carp's barbels. Scale and ray counts overlap with those of the parents, but pharyngeal teeth number 3+1+1, 4+1+1, 2+1+1, 3+1 or 4+1 (on either side).

Rudd x dace

Slimmer than the rudd with flattened sides, this hybrid has a terminal mouth with level upper and lower lips. It is silver in colour and has a yellow tinge. The front of the dorsal fin base is a short distance only behind the pelvic fin. Fin ray and scale counts overlap and are of no help in identifying this hybrid, but the pharyngeal teeth appear distinct. The count is like its parents – 5+2 (or 3) : 2 (or 3)+5 – but the teeth are weakly hooked and have slight serrations.

Rudd x bream

This is a beautiful fish in larger sizes, when it is often light golden-brown. It is very deep-bodied with a distinctly keeled belly and lower lip that projects slightly in front of the upper lip. The number of branched rays in its anal fin are diagnostic (15–19).

Rudd x silver bream

Deep-bodied and silver like the silver bream, the rudd x silver bream hybrid has less of a 'humped back' appearance and smaller eyes than its parent species. Its mouth is terminal and level, and the fins tend to be orange or reddish in colour, especially the pelvic and pectoral fins, and they lack the grey tips of the silver bream. The ray count in the anal fin of this fish is normally diagnostic (range 12–18, but rarely less than 15). The pharyngeal teeth will be the same as one of its parents, but they will be weakly serrated.

Rudd x bleak

This hybrid resembles the bleak, but has a slightly deeper body, smaller eyes and an orange tinge to its fins, especially the pelvic and anal fins. The anal fin ray count is a useful feature in many specimens (13–15, mostly 14–15). The pharyngeal teeth will be the same as one of its parents and they will be strongly serrated.

Bream x silver bream

Resembling the silver bream in overall shape and coloration, this hybrid has red pectoral and pelvic fins and its body is noticeably slimy, similar to that of the bream. The pharyngeal teeth are mostly the same as those of the silver bream, but some are 5+2 : 2+5.

Bleak x chub
Bleak x dace
Bleak x silver bream

These hybrids grow larger than the bleak, but they retain the upturned jaw and large eyes of the bleak. The number of rays in the anal fin are diagnostic (11–14).

The following hybrids have been reported from European freshwaters, but no description has been seen, nor has the author examined a specimen:

Roach x chub
Rudd x chub
Dace x bream
Ide x unspecified cyprinids

Stone Loach *Noemacheilus (Barbatula) barbatula*

Loaches are small, slender, bottom-dwelling fish that superficially could be confused with gudgeon or very small barbel. However, the loach's fins lack spines and it always has more than two pairs of barbels around the mouth.

Short-based, yellow-buff dorsal fin with dark spotting and 9–11 rays

Brown-olive or dirty yellow-brown back

Shallow-forked, buff-yellow tail fin with dark spotting and rounded corners

Light yellow-brown sides with irregular dark grey-brown blotches

Short-based, yellow-buff anal fin with dark spotting and 7–10 rays

Fairly small head

Pale yellow belly

Dark spots on yellow-buff pelvic and pectoral fins

Underslung mouth has six barbels (four in front; two at corners)

c.10cm

Distribution

The stone loach occurs in clean rivers and some lakes from the Pyrenees eastwards to Russia, but not in the far north. It has been introduced to waters where it does not naturally occur by anglers who use them as bait for trout.

The stone loach's elongated body is rounded between the head and dorsal fin, but flattened along each side of the tail. Its head is fairly small and the underslung mouth has six barbels – four in front and one at each corner. The short-based dorsal fin is opposite the pelvic fins and born midway along the body; the short-based anal fin is midway between the pelvic and tail fins. The tail fin has a very shallow fork and rounded corners.

Its scales are very small, the lateral line is distinct only at the front of the body and it is covered with thick slime.

Coloration is camouflaged for life on the bottom of rivers and lakes. The back is usually brown-olive or dirty yellow-brown, the sides are a lighter yellow-brown, irregularly blotched dark grey-brown, and the belly is a pale yellow buff. All the fins have a yellow-buff background, there are a few dark spots on the pectoral and pelvic fins and similar spotting is arranged as bands close to the fin edge on the dorsal, anal and tail fins.

Both sexes develop minute tubercles on their pectoral fins when they first breed and adult males usually retain these (females have them for the breeding season only).

Breeding behaviour and life cycle

The breeding season starts in late April or early May and continues through the summer until August. The female chooses a position where she will deposit her eggs, which might be a hidden nest in a hollow beneath a boulder or a hollow in gravel or in a patch of dense weed. Here she lays a batch of 1mm-diameter, yellow, sticky eggs, which are then fertilised by the male. The female guards the eggs or at least remains in their vicinity until they hatch about two weeks later. Initially stone loach larvae are about 3mm long and lack barbels, but after about five weeks, when they are about 15mm long, barbels begin to develop. The fry keep together in dense shoals throughout the summer of their birth, remaining mainly in very shallow water where aquatic predators rarely venture.

Once one batch of eggs has developed, an adult female will lay another so that, over a complete breeding season, she may produce four or more broods or a total of over 10,000 eggs.

The stone loach is perfectly camouflaged among stones.

Food and feeding behaviour

Although stone loach fry commonly feed throughout bright summer days, older fish are usually nocturnal feeders, hiding buried in mud or weeds, or among rocks during the day. They do venture out, but only in overcast weather or when the river is murky.

Studies have demonstrated that, in the summer and autumn after they hatch, juvenile stone loaches tend to feed on different organisms than older fish, including foods that swim just off the bottom. They consume large amounts of microscopic algae and planktonic crustaceans, especially ostracods, although lake populations also take copepods and cladocerans in large quantities. Blackfly larvae and pupae are also important in the juvenile diet in rivers.

Adults are entirely bottom-feeders, taking a wide variety of river or lake bed invertebrates that they find with their barbels and sensitive lips. Midge larvae and pupae often dominate the diet, but when freshwater shrimps, and mayfly and stonefly nymphs are abundant, they will eat these.

Growth and longevity

The stone loach grows to 8–12cm after two to three years, and exceptionally to 15cm after seven years. They mature at the end of their first year.

Predators

Kingfishers feed their chicks on growing stone loach fry (98 per cent of prey fed to chicks by one pair was stone loaches); goosanders hunt them; and herons will sometimes stand in the shallows and take well-grown juveniles one after the other (one grey heron took 47 in one hour, and another took 71 in 64 minutes!). Stone loach are important in the diet of many aquatic fish including brown and rainbow trout, chub, asp, burbot, large miller's thumb, perch and eels.

Conservation status of stone loach
Organic pollution, which creates low levels of oxygen in the water, can be tolerated by some fish species but not the stone loach. As such, this species has been lost from some river stretches. Where the water remains clean the stone loach is an abundant species. Most naturalists use the presence or absence of salmonids as an indication of clean or polluted waters, but because this species requires cleaner water than even trout and salmon, it is a better indicator of clean, unpolluted water.

Pond Loach *Misgurnus fossilis*

The pond loach is well camouflaged for a life spent at the bottom of murky ponds. It occurs in small, stagnant lowland pools with low oxygen levels.

Light yellow-brown fins with darker patches that sometimes form bands, particularly on the tail fin

Drab brown or yellow-brown back shading to sandy sides

Lines or stripes break up into spots along tail

Short-based dorsal fin with 5–7 rays

Small, rounded anal fin with 5–6 rays

Distinct dark grey-brown stripe along sides

Body covered in thick slime

Small head

Orange-brown belly

Tiny scales

Ventral mouth with 10 barbels (four on snout tip, four on lower jaw and one at each corner of mouth)

← c.20–25cm →

Distribution

This species occurs from France eastwards to Russia. As well as surviving in badly oxygenated water, the pond loach is the only European fish that can survive a temporary drought. If the water level falls dangerously low, it burrows deep into mud where, surrounded by a mass of slime, the fish aestivates until rain brings fresh water and the pond begins to fill.

The pond loach is one of several European fish that is rarely seen or appreciated by naturalists and anglers.

Growth and longevity

The pond loach is the largest European loach. After one year it averages about 6cm, after two years about 12cm, after three years 20cm, and after four years 25cm. It may grow, exceptionally, to 35cm. It matures at three to four years.

Predators

The pond loach's nocturnal behaviour makes it almost impossible for diurnal predators to catch them and the almost anaerobic nature of its habitat prevents predatory fish living with it.

Coping with low oxygen levels in the water

Should water oxygen levels fall to almost zero, the pond loach can breathe atmospheric air; it swims to the surface, takes a gulp of air into its mouth and swallows it. The gut, which has a specially folded lining to enhance oxygen absorption, then absorbs the oxygen from the air. This is different to the strategy used by the European mudminnow and crucian carp, which obtain oxygen via their gills.

An alternative name of the pond loach is the 'weatherfish', because of the way it can react to changes in weather. In hot thundery conditions, when the amount of oxygen held by the water may decrease suddenly, pond loach move to the surface and take in air. In hot droughts they bury themselves in the bottom and remain in a state of torpor.

The pond loach has a long, slender body, rounded in cross section, but flattened immediately in front of the tail fin. The head is small with a ventral mouth that has 10 barbels (four on the tip of the snout, which includes the two longest, four on the lower jaw, which are tiny and difficult to see, and one at each corner of the mouth).

The very short-based, small dorsal and pelvic fins are opposite; they are born nearer to the tail fin than the head. The anal fin is small, rounded and set slightly closer to the pelvic fin than the anal fin base. The lateral line is distinct only at the front of the body and the scales are very tiny. The body is covered with thick slime.

The coloration of its back is a drab brown or yellow-brown, shading down the sides to sandy brown or orange-brown on the belly. A distinct dark grey-brown stripe runs along the sides of its body and other similar, but less distinct, lines or stripes break up into spots along the tail. The fins are usually a light yellow-brown with darker speckling sometimes arranged as bands, especially on the tail fin. Adult males have tiny tubercles on their pectoral fins.

Breeding behaviour and life cycle

The pond loach begins to spawn in late March and, if the pond has not dried out (see Distribution left), it will continue to spawn until late June or early July. The female chooses a growth of water weed and lays a batch of 1.5mm-diameter, red-brown eggs, which stick to the weed. The eggs are immediately fertilised by an accompanying male. A female will produce other batches at intervals over several weeks until she is spent. The total number of eggs laid by one female pond loach is estimated to be over 50,000 and may be as many as 150,000.

The eggs hatch after about 10 days and the 3–4mm larvae have long, thread-like, external gills that help them extract oxygen from the water. Pond loach larvae lack barbels, but these develop as the tiny fish grows. They are fully developed after about two months when the juvenile pond loach has grown to about 2.5cm.

Food and feeding behaviour

Pond loaches hide buried in mud or weed during the day. They feed at night entirely on the pond bed. Larvae and juveniles eat large quantities of very small crustaceans; the slightly larger crustaceans, copepods and cladocerans, become important in the diet later.

Adult pond loaches eat whatever they can root out from the bottom of the pond, using their barbels and lips to feel and identify suitable food, such as small pond snails, pea-mussels, water hog-lice, midge larvae and small worms.

Conservation status of pond loach

There is no doubt that the population of this species is greatly under-recorded, partly because of its nocturnal habits and partly because few naturalists research the bottom of shallow, stagnant pools. When two pools in Holland, five in Denmark and four in northern Poland were sampled, pond loaches were found in eight. However, widespread marsh and pond drainage and the destruction of weedy ditches has caused pond loach populations to decline across the European range.

Spined Loach *Cobitis taenia*

This little fish is widespread throughout much of Europe, but it is rarely seen and its lifestyle has been poorly studied. It can live in stagnant water, where oxygen levels fall to nearly zero, by gulping air at the surface.

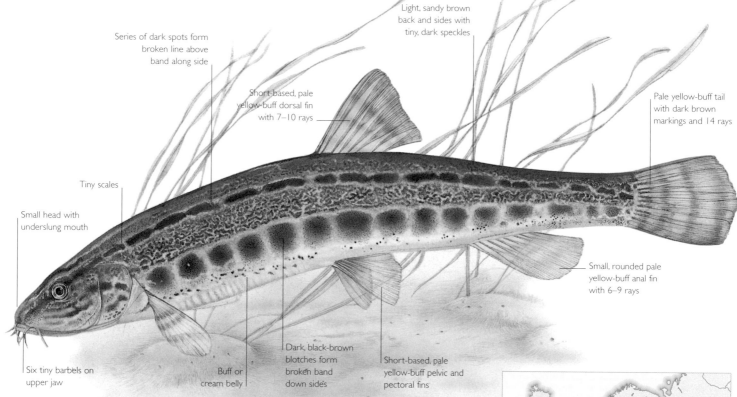

Series of dark spots form broken line above band along side

Light, sandy brown back and sides with tiny, dark speckles

Short-based, pale yellow-buff dorsal fin with 7–10 rays

Pale yellow-buff tail with dark brown markings and 14 rays

Tiny scales

Small head with underslung mouth

Six tiny barbels on upper jaw

Buff or cream belly

Dark, black-brown blotches form broken band down sides

Short-based, pale yellow-buff pelvic and pectoral fins

Small, rounded pale yellow-buff anal fin with 6–9 rays

← c.5–10cm →

Distribution

The spined loach is found in mud- or fine silt-bottomed slow rivers, canals and lakes throughout most of Europe except for northerly regions. The Spanish population has been separated into two different species by some scientists: Cobitis calderoni *in the north of Spain and* C. maroccana *in the south. Similarly the Romanian population has been named* Sabanejewia romanica *and Italian* S. larvata.

Growth and longevity

The spined loach grows to an average length of about 5cm, and exceptionally 10–12cm, after two years.

Predators

The spined loach's nocturnal behaviour will hinder diurnal predators, although crepuscular-feeding herons, chub, perch and zander probably eat them occasionally.

Related species

The Balkan loach (Cobitis elongata) is very similar to the spined loach, but its tail is more elongated and the anal fin is slightly nearer the pelvic fins than the tail fin (midway in spined loach). There is a distinct, unbroken brown-black line running through a series of round spots along its sides from the gills to the base of the tail fin. The Balkan loach is, on average, a little bigger than the spined loach, with an average length of about 10cm and a maximum length of 15–16cm. It lives in slow streams that drain in the Balkans.
Ray count: tail 14.

The golden loach (Cobitis aurata), although very similar to the spined loach, has warm yellow- or golden-brown sides with a single line of large, dark brown spots and numerous tiny speckles. It grows to an average length of approximately 9cm, with a maximum of 12cm. Golden loach are found in the River Danube and other rivers that drain into the Black and Caspian Seas.
Ray count: tail 12–13.

Conservation status of spined loach

The abundance of this species is not well known because it is so secretive and difficult to sample with a pond-net or bottle trap. However, determined efforts to sample the species in two Swiss, one Slovenian and two French rivers were all successful, suggesting that the spined loach is thriving throughout its range.

The spined loach has an elongated body that is laterally flattened along its entire length. It has a small head and an underslung mouth with six extremely small barbels on the upper jaw (four to the front and one in each corner). A small, two-pointed spine is held in a groove below the eye; this is inconspicuous, but you can feel it if you run your finger very gently forwards along the side of the fish's head.

The pelvic and short-based dorsal fins are opposite and are held midway along the body. The anal fin is small and rounded and positioned midway between pelvic and tail fins. The scales are tiny and although it is slimy, this species is usually far less slimy than the previous two loaches.

The back and sides are a light, sandy brown with tiny, darker speckles. Darker, black-brown blotches form a broken band down the sides and a series of dark spots forms a broken line above this band. The belly is buff or cream. The pectoral, pelvic and anal fins are a pale yellow-buff and usually unmarked; the dorsal and tail fins are pale yellow-buff with dark brown markings.

Breeding behaviour and life cycle

Very little is known about the spined loach's life cycle, but it spawns between April and June. The female deposits 6000–8000, 1mm-diameter, pale

The spined loach is perfectly camouflaged on the bottom of silt or muddy waters.

yellow, sticky eggs in cavities among stones or on vegetation. It is not known whether she lays further egg batches. The eggs hatch after 10 to 14 days and the 3mm-long larvae begin to feed on microscopic food particles that they ingest with mud (see below).

Food and feeding behaviour

Spined loaches lie buried in mud during daylight with the tops of their heads and eyes at the surface. It is certain that they do not use their eyes to spot food, and probable that their main use is to detect when the sun goes down, for spined loaches are nocturnal feeders.

Although adults will pick up individual food items, such as bloodworms, from the bottom, all ages eat most of their food by filtering mud. Mud is taken into the mouth and food items, such as rotifers, tiny crustaceans, and small insect larvae and worms, are passed back into the gut and the filtered mud spat out. How the separation of mud and food is achieved is not known for certain, but it is thought that food items become stuck to mucus in the mouth and the mucus and food are swallowed.

European Catfish *Siluris glanis*

This predatory and quite ugly species is the largest, permanently resident freshwater fish in Europe. It occurs in muddy- or silt-bottomed lakes and slow, deep, lowland rivers.

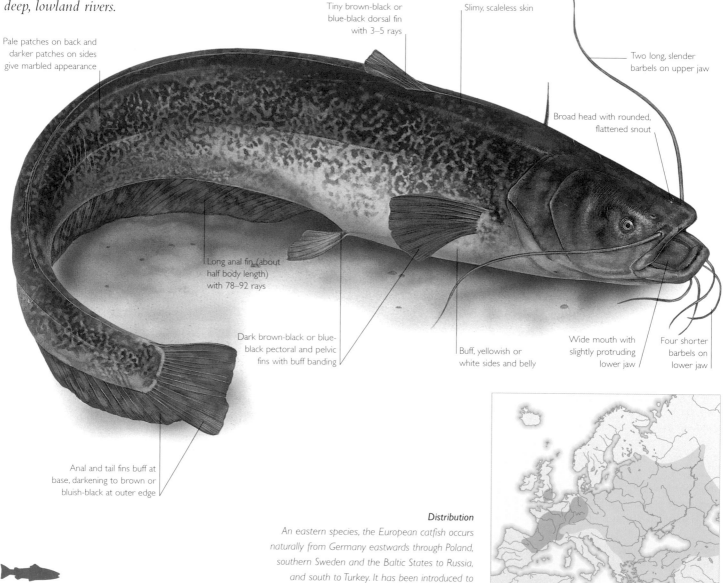

Pale patches on back and darker patches on sides give marbled appearance

Tiny brown-black or blue-black dorsal fin with 3–5 rays

Slimy, scaleless skin

Two long, slender barbels on upper jaw

Broad head with rounded, flattened snout

Long anal fin (about half body length) with 78–92 rays

Dark brown-black or blue-black pectoral and pelvic fins with buff banding

Buff, yellowish or white sides and belly

Wide mouth with slightly protruding lower jaw

Four shorter barbels on lower jaw

Anal and tail fins buff at base, darkening to brown or bluish-black at outer edge

← c.1m+ →

Distribution

An eastern species, the European catfish occurs naturally from Germany eastwards through Poland, southern Sweden and the Baltic States to Russia, and south to Turkey. It has been introduced to England, Italy, France and Spain.

This huge fish is easily identified by its elongated, stout body and very broad head with rounded, flattened snout. Its eyes are minute with a white iris and black pupil. The mouth is very wide with a slightly protruding lower jaw; the upper jaw bears two long, slender barbels, the lower jaw four shorter barbels. The dorsal fin is tiny; the anal fin is very long (about half its body length) and ends just before the tail fin. The scaleless skin is slimy.

The coloration is variable: the back may be black, deep violet, dark olive-green or red-brown; the sides and belly may be drab buff, yellowish or white. The back has paler patches, the sides and belly darker ones, often giving a marbled appearance. The pectoral and pelvic fins are dark brown-black or blue-black with buff-yellow banding and, in larger specimens, red edges. The dorsal fin is brown-black or blue-black. The anal and tail fins are drab buff at the base, darkening to brown or bluish-black at the outer edge.

Breeding behaviour and life cycle

This species will not breed until the water temperature has reached at least 20°C, which is in mid-May to June in the south of its range and July to August in the north. The male excavates a redd in weedy gravel or sand-bottomed shallows into which the female deposits a clump of relatively large (3mm-diameter), yellow, sticky eggs. The number of eggs produced depends on the size of the female and is equivalent to 25,000–30,000 per kilogram of her weight.

After fertilising the eggs the male guards them until they hatch – usually three to four days later at water temperatures of 20–21°C. When newly hatched, larval catfish are about 7mm long and have one barbel. They remain in the redd, guarded by the male, until their yolk sacs have been fully absorbed. They then disperse to feed on invertebrates close to the bottom. They become piscivorous at about the end of their first year when they have grown to 20–25cm.

Food and feeding behaviour

The catfish is a solitary feeder and mainly crepuscular or nocturnal. Its main food is other fish and its diet includes tench, bream, rudd and roach, eels and burbot. It will also eat water voles, brown rats, ducklings and moorhen chicks, amphibians and crayfish. There are reports of children and dogs being attacked in the water. The catfish feeds from spring to the end of autumn and hibernates in deep holes, among tree roots or under bank overhangs, during winter.

The immense size of this fish and its carnivorous reputation makes catching one an angler's crowning glory. Not surprisingly, several incredible baits have been used, including whole rabbits, half-plucked hens and ducks, suckling pigs and big lumps of meat. The European catfish's staggering power is best illustrated by the true story of a Polish youth who free-lined a bait from his rowing boat, tying the end of his line to his arm. A catfish took the bait, dragged him from his boat and towed him down into the depths where he drowned.

Growth and longevity

Growth rate depends on the abundance of food and length of the warm-water feeding season. In optimal conditions European catfish will reach about 50cm long and 2kg in weight after four to five years (when they spawn for the first time); and 1m and 10kg after nine to 10 years. They may live for 15 to 20 years (exceptionally to 30 years)

A catfish emerging from its lair, which is found among boulders on a lake bed.

and to huge sizes: 2–3m long weighing up to 200kg, with exceptional reports of 5m and 306kg. However, in cooler conditions, where food is less abundant, a 10-year-old catfish may weigh only 2kg. Males are larger than females of the same age. The record caught by an angler (from the River Danube, Romania) weighed a mighty 91.82kg and took five hours to land.

Predators

Although catfish fry might be eaten by other fish, such as pike, once they have grown to a reasonable size humans are their only predators.

> *Conservation status of European catfish*
> *The population appears to be stable in most regions and is probably regulated by the amount of food available. The trend to introduce this species into waters where it does not naturally occur is worrying because it will almost certainly have a great impact on the populations of native fish, waterfowl, amphibians and aquatic mammals.*

Three-spined Stickleback *Gasterosteus aculeatus*

This is one of Europe's best-known fish and is usually the first to be caught by children dipping a pond-net or dangling a glass jar into a pond.

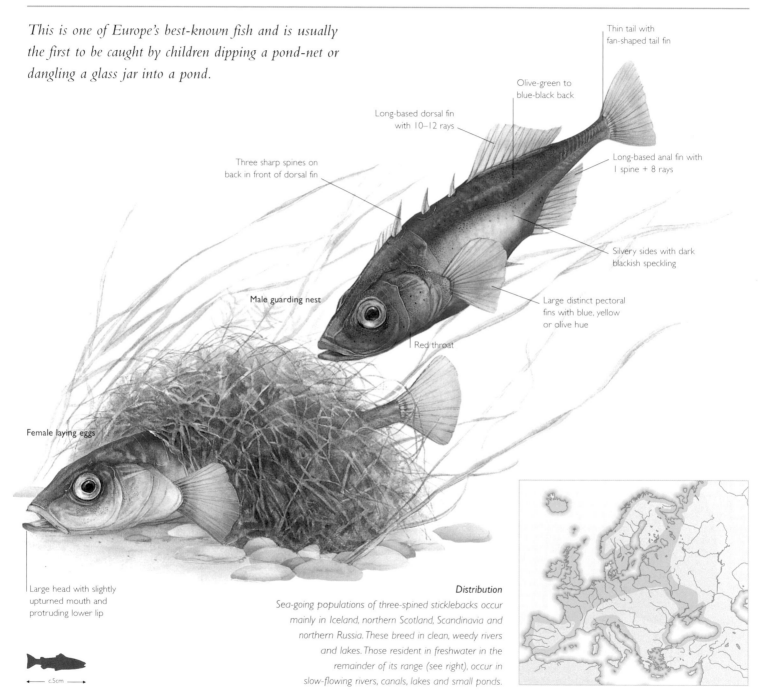

Thin tail with fan-shaped tail fin

Olive-green to blue-black back

Long-based dorsal fin with 10–12 rays

Three sharp spines on back in front of dorsal fin

Long-based anal fin with 1 spine + 8 rays

Silvery sides with dark blackish speckling

Large distinct pectoral fins with blue, yellow or olive hue

Red throat

Male guarding nest

Female laying eggs

Large head with slightly upturned mouth and protruding lower lip

c.5cm

Distribution

Sea-going populations of three-spined sticklebacks occur mainly in Iceland, northern Scotland, Scandinavia and northern Russia. These breed in clean, weedy rivers and lakes. Those resident in freshwater in the remainder of its range (see right), occur in slow-flowing rivers, canals, lakes and small ponds.

The three-spined stickleback is a tiny fish with a moderately deep body, flattened along the sides, which tapers at the rear to a thin tail, terminating in a fan-shaped tail fin. The large head is pointed with a slightly upturned, large mouth and a slightly protruding lower lip. There are three (occasionally two) sharp spines on the back in front of the long-based dorsal fin. The pectoral fins are large and conspicuous; the pelvic fins are reduced to a single sharp spine and a tiny ray; and the anal fin is long-based and positioned opposite the dorsal fin. The body is scaleless, but has bony plates or 'scutes' and variations in the number of these plates has given rise to varietal names:

• *trachurus* has up to 25 plates along the sides of the body and up to eight tiny platelets along the tail. It is the common form in northernmost areas (Iceland, Scandinavia, rivers draining into the Arctic Ocean) and it migrates to sea more than the other forms.

• *leiurus* is plateless or has a very few plates at the front of the body. It is the commoner form in the remainder of Europe and tends not to migrate to sea.

• *semiarmatus* has a few plates at the front of the body and at the base of the tail close to the tail fin. This form is considered a hybrid of the other two forms and is commonest at the boundary between *trachurus* and *leiurus*. It probably does not go to sea.

Coloration of three-spined sticklebacks is variable: olive-green to blue-black on the back, silvery with dark blackish specklings on the sides and whitish (often with a blue, yellow or olive hue) on the belly.

Sea-going sticklebacks are generally more silvery than those that remain in freshwater all year round. In the breeding season the male attains a brilliant mating dress with bright red throat and belly and blue eyes.

Breeding behaviour and life cycle

In the north of the range a large proportion of the population is migratory, moving downstream in autumn to estuaries, fjords and the open sea. Return migration occurs in spring. In the rest of the range some sticklebacks may move

downstream as far as brackish saltmarsh creeks and harbours, but most remain in freshwater. Three-spined sticklebacks breed from mid-March to June, in shallow, weedy water.

The male builds a nest of weed, about 5cm in diameter, which is glued together using secretions from his kidney. He guards his nest and surrounding territory from other males. A ripe female is attracted to the nest by the male's intricate zig-zag dance at the end of which she follows him into the nest. Here she lays up to about 100, 1.5mm-diameter, yellow eggs, which the male then fertilises before driving the female away. Most females lay their eggs in batches, in the nest of the same or a different male.

The male guards the eggs until they hatch up to four weeks later, depending on water temperature (only six to seven days at 18°C), fanning them with his pectoral fins to ensure a constant flow of oxygenated water.

After hatching, the young remain in the nest for a further five to eight days, guarded by the male, before dispersing.

Food and feeding behaviour

Three-spined sticklebacks devour a wide range of aquatic invertebrates, including planktonic crustaceans, midge larvae, water hog-lice and small snails and worms. They will also eat the eggs

A male stickleback in his gaudy spawning coloration.

and tiny fry of other fish. When not breeding they are shoal fish and they will often join together to attack and pull apart potential food that is too large for one to swallow whole.

Growth and longevity

Most three-spined sticklebacks reach 4–5cm in length at the end of one to two years, when they mature. The maximum length achieved in freshwater populations (including aquarium fish) is 5–8cm at three years old, up to 11cm in migratory populations.

Predators

Three-spined sticklebacks are taken by a wide range of predators including birds, such as kingfishers and perch. Both take care to ensure that the stickleback is swallowed head-first so that the it slides down to the stomach easily. If swallowed tail-first, the spines would catch in the predator's oesophagus, with painful consequences.

Conservation status of three-spined stickleback
This fish species is normally abundant throughout its range.

Miller's Thumb *Cottus gobio*

So called because it was said to resemble a corn miller's thumb, swollen through testing the texture of flour, the miller's thumb is one of the characteristic small fish of clean, boulder-strewn rivers and lakes.

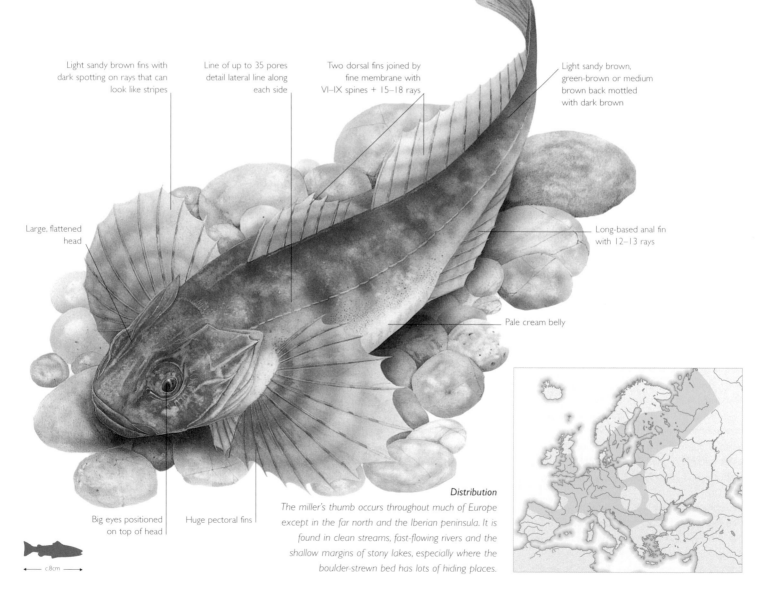

Light sandy brown fins with dark spotting on rays that can look like stripes

Line of up to 35 pores detail lateral line along each side

Two dorsal fins joined by fine membrane with VI–IX spines + 15–18 rays

Light sandy brown, green-brown or medium brown back mottled with dark brown

Large, flattened head

Long-based anal fin with 12–13 rays

Pale cream belly

Big eyes positioned on top of head

Huge pectoral fins

c.8cm

Distribution

The miller's thumb occurs throughout much of Europe except in the far north and the Iberian peninsula. It is found in clean streams, fast-flowing rivers and the shallow margins of stony lakes, especially where the boulder-strewn bed has lots of hiding places.

This small, bottom-dwelling and superficially ugly fish has a fairly stout, tapering, scaleless body, a large flattened head with big eyes and huge fins. The eyes are held on top of the head, which is an adaptation to life on the bottom, and they have a complex double cornea giving protection against moving sand and gravel particles in a swift river.

Two dorsal fins, joined by a fine membrane, run almost the entire length of the back, the anal fin is very long-based and the pectoral fins are huge. The pelvic fins are carried well forward with their bases below the pectoral fin bases. The lateral line is present as a line of up to about 35 pores running along the sides.

Coloration is generally light sandy brown, green-brown or medium brown, mottled with dark brown on the back, and the belly is pale cream. The fins are light sandy brown with dark spotting on rays giving a striped effect, except for the pelvic fins, which lack darker markings.

Breeding behaviour and life cycle

In the south of its range the miller's thumb spawns from February to April; in the north March to June. Occasionally the fish will have two spawning periods, the later one in July.

The male finds a suitable hollow under a boulder or excavates a hollow. Courtship then follows, when a female is enticed to join the male in his nest and spawn with him: she lays a mass of up to about 300 relatively large, 2.5mm-diameter, sticky, yellowish eggs and the male fertilises them. The male guards the eggs ferociously until they hatch three to four weeks later into 6–7mm-long larvae, which still have large yolk sacs. They remain in the nest for another 10 to 12 days, guarded by the male, until their yolk sacs are exhausted. Then, measuring 6–7mm, the fry disperse.

Food and feeding behaviour

A nocturnal feeder, hiding under stones during the day, the miller's thumb feeds on any animal foods it can catch and swallow, which is often a representative sample of what happens to be most abundant in the water – it is an opportunistic feeder. In one river, for example, mayfly and stonefly nymphs and caddis and midge larvae formed the bulk of this species' diet, but with a sudden spring explosion of the *Gammarus* (freshwater shrimp) population the miller's thumb turned entirely to them. By summer, when the *Gammarus* population had fallen, nymphs and larvae again dominated the diet.

During a spate, this fish will feed on washed-out earthworms, slugs and insect larvae. In autumn they will gorge on salmon and trout eggs washed from redds upstream, and in spring and summer they will catch small fry that stray close. Feeding slows in winter and, with water temperatures close to freezing, this fish hides under boulders.

Growth and longevity

After one year miller's thumbs reach 4–5cm in length, 6–8cm after two years and a maximum size of 8–10cm after three years. Females are usually larger than males of the same age and both sexes mature at two to three years of age. There are reports of fish reaching 16cm in subarctic waters.

Predators

This is one of the main foods of large predatory trout as the trout feed at night when the miller's thumb is most active. It is also a food for grey herons, kingfishers, goosanders, otters and feral

The miller's thumb, also sometimes called sculpin, is a river or lake-bed fish that rarely rises off the bottom.

American mink. From 1962–65, one pair of tawny owls, nesting close to a river, fed their young entirely on this species and raised 19 chicks.

Conservation status of miller's thumb

This fish was once abundant, but in many rivers siltation (following land drainage) and reduced flows (following water abstraction in upland rivers) has caused a population collapse. Boulders have become covered in fine sediments and the river bed concreted so that the miller's thumb has nowhere to hide or excavate its nest. In one river in northern England where, in 1970–71, there was an average of 3.8 miller's thumbs per square metre of river, there was only 0.3 per square metre in 1995. In another river, mean density has fallen from 1.9 per square metre to 0.4; and in one tiny stream 3m wide, where there was an average of 3.8 fish per metre in 1969, there was none over a 2.1km stretch in 1997. Happily, in wilder areas, the species still thrives.

Bass *Dicentrarchus labrax*

The French refer to the bass as the 'wolf of the sea'
because of its reputation of hounding shoals of lesser fish
in a pack. Although it is a saltwater species, the bass does
penetrate dilute, brackish water at the heads of estuaries.

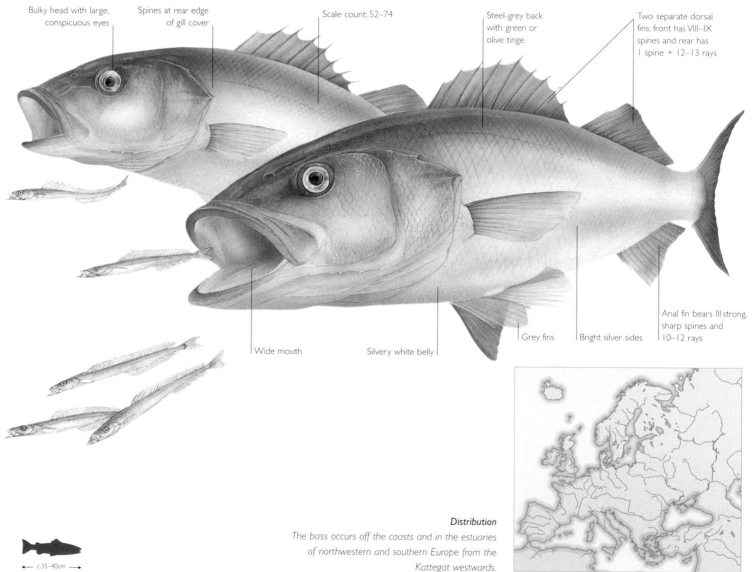

Bulky head with large, conspicuous eyes

Spines at rear edge of gill cover

Scale count: 52–74

Steel-grey back with green or olive tinge

Two separate dorsal fins; front has VIII–IX spines and rear has 1 spine + 12–13 rays

Wide mouth

Silvery white belly

Grey fins

Bright silver sides

Anal fin bears III strong, sharp spines and 10–12 rays

← c.35–40cm →

Distribution
The bass occurs off the coasts and in the estuaries
of northwestern and southern Europe from the
Kattegat westwards.

The sea-silvery bass is a gourmet's delight, and its future depends on sensible fisheries management.

The body is slender, streamlined and powerfully built with a maximum body width at the shoulders. It has a relatively bulky head, large, conspicuous eyes and a wide mouth. The gill cover has strong, sharp, forward-pointing spines below the eyes and there are two flat spines at the rear edge. The two dorsal fins are separate and the front dorsal fin and anal fin bear strong, sharp spines. (Take care when handling bass.)

Overall coloration is bright, silvery and unspotted: the back is steel-grey with a green or olive tinge, the sides are bright silver and the belly is silvery white. The fins are grey.

Breeding behaviour and life cycle

Bass spawn during March to May in deep, inshore seas. Adults gather in large shoals and the females release huge numbers of eggs, equivalent to 250,000–500,000 per kilogram of their body weight. The transparent, 1.5mm-diameter eggs contain minute, clear globules of oil and so their density is less than that of seawater and they float to the surface and drift with the currents.

After one week the 3–4mm larvae emerge and drift in the surface layer of the sea as part of the zooplankton. The larvae feed on the plankton around them until they are about 2–3cm long. They then swim inshore to seek larger foods.

After breeding the adults remain inshore feeding, often entering estuaries with the tide. They tend to retreat southwestwards in autumn to winter in warmer waters. In recent years some bass have wintered in the north of their range, usually close to industrial outfalls (see below).

Food and feeding behaviour

Bass shoals feed mainly on small fish, such as sand eels, sprats and fry, crabs, shrimps and prawns. Most feeding occurs with the tide and feeding intensity is greater at tides that peak at dusk, at night and at dawn rather than during the day.

The bass follow the rising tide in estuaries, feeding in shallow water on the slopes of recently flooded sand banks, moving quickly upstream as their fish or crustacean prey moves onto the next flooding bank. Eventually they may almost enter freshwater: in one river in England they have been recorded taking small roach and dace.

Three bass feeding hot-spots are the tide rips around a steep bank, sea wall or jetty; where a side stream enters an estuary and provides shelter for lesser fry; and warm water industrial outfalls that attract masses of lesser fry. When the water cools in autumn many bass move to deeper water or head to the milder southwest, but some remain feeding through the winter in warm-water outfalls.

Growth and longevity

The bass is a slow-growing, but potentially long-lived fish. At the end of its first year, it will be about 10–12cm, at the end of the second year 15–20cm and at three years old it reaches about 25cm. Some bass breed for the first time when they are four years old, but most wait until they are five or six, about 35cm (males) or 40cm (females) long and weighing upwards of 1.5kg. After 20 years bass can be quite heavy – 5–6kg, exceptionally to 9kg – but in many areas bass are caught before they can grow to this large size. Most bass caught today weigh 1–2kg.

Predators

Cormorants and grey herons take some bass in estuaries, but humans are by far the greatest predators of adult bass.

Related species

The spotted bass (Dicentrarchus punctatus) is a less widespread species, occurring along the coasts from France, south around Spain and Portugal, and along the western Mediterranean to Italy. It is easily identified by its black-spotted sides and by the comb-like margins of the scales found on its head between the eyes.

Conservation status of bass

Because it is so highly prized as food (it is among the most expensive of all fish) it is intensively fished for. The consequence of this is that, while small, immature bass are fairly plentiful, older, larger specimens that have spawned several times are now quite rare. A sensible bass fisheries management would ensure that if large bass are caught, they are returned alive so they can spawn, and a sensible harvest is taken from immature fish. The bass has been excluded from many estuaries by pollution.

Largemouth Bass *Micropterus salmoides*

The largemouth bass is a North American fish with a high reputation among anglers: it is a predator that will take an angler's fly or bait fiercely.

A fairly stocky fish with a stout body, the largemouth bass has a double, but united, dorsal fin. The front part is supported by stout spines and the second by soft rays. The anal fin has three to seven spines at the front. Its body is fully scaled and the lateral line is complete.

Breeding behaviour and life cycle

Spawning occurs when the water temperature exceeds 18°C. The male establishes a territory, usually in shallow, weedy water, and excavates a hollow. Other males are chased from the nest site, whereas passing females are chased to the site to lay a batch of eggs. Each female produces an equivalent of 1000–3000 eggs per kilogram of her body weight. The eggs are 1.5mm in diameter, light orange-yellow and sticky. The male guards the nest and keeps a fresh supply of water flowing over the eggs by fanning them. The tiny larvae hatch after about five days and leave the nest about a week later. The male keeps his brood together as a shoal, often for many weeks, before leaving them.

Food and feeding behaviour

Fry eat invertebrates, but adults are predatory, eating mainly lesser fish and amphibians, which they ambush. They almost stop feeding when water temperature falls below about 8°C.

Growth and longevity

Growth depends on water temperature and food availability. In warm, productive waters, they may grow to 10cm before the first winter, then growth continues rapidly to 40–50cm, exceptionally 80cm. They often live for 10 years or more.

Predators

Perch and other small piscivores probably eat huge numbers of fry. The adults' lies probably shield them from most predators except large pike.

Distribution and habitat

Introduced to lakes and canals in France, Germany, Belgium, Holland and England, this species' temperature requirements will hinder its spread.

Conservation status of largemouth bass
In some areas there is concern that the largemouth bass will damage native fish stocks, and care should be taken before introducing it to a new water.

Two dorsal fins separated by a deep notch; front has IX–X spines and rear has I spine + 12–13 rays

Scale count: 60–70

Small fish have dusky grey markings on sides that may appear as a faint stripe

Dark olive or olive-green overall coloration

Prominent eyes

Huge mouth

Jaw extends back to beyond rear of eye

Large head (tip of snout to rear of gill cover is greater than depth of body)

Anal fin has III spines + 10–11 rays

Golden-olive sides

Whitish belly

c.40cm

Smallmouth Bass *Micropterus dolomieu*

The smallmouth bass is a close relation of the largemouth bass and was also introduced from North America.

Related species
The rock bass (Ambloplites rupestris) was introduced to an unknown number of European lakes and canals. The pumpkinseed (Lepomis gibbosus) was released into canals and lakes in northwest Europe, north to England and Poland. The green sunfish (Lepomis cyanellus) was introduced to western Germany. The red-breasted sunfish (Lepomis auritus) was introduced to central Italy.

Conservation status of smallmouth bass
Introducing this fish could damage stocks of native fish – no more should be introduced.

With its stocky, stout body, large head and conspicuous double dorsal fin this species is very similar to the largemouth bass. There are, however, distinct differences, such as the length of the upper jaw, the number of scales in the lateral line, the shape of the dorsal fin and overall coloration.

Breeding behaviour and life cycle
Spawning occurs from late April to June, occasionally into July, when the water temperature exceeds 15°C. Males become territorial, choosing a patch of river or lake bed covered by clean sand or fine gravel. He excavates a shallow nest to which he then shepherds passing ripe females. They shed 5000–15,000, yellowish, 1.5mm diameter eggs, which the male fertilises and guards from predators, including other smallmouth bass.

The eggs hatch after about five days and the 3–4mm-long larvae leave the nest about a week later. The male continues to guard the tiny fish for several days, sometimes weeks, before they become independent as fry.

Food and feeding behaviour
Smallmouth bass fry eat invertebrates, but soon turn to a diet of fish, amphibians and larger crustaceans. Feeding intensity declines in autumn as water temperatures dip below about 12°C, and feeding ceases below about 6°C.

Growth and longevity
In warm waters where potential prey is abundant, this fish grows to about 10cm long before its first winter. It matures at three to four years old at an average length of 30–35cm. Large specimens may reach 50cm and live for about 10 years.

Predators
Perch and pike, together with other smallmouth bass, are probably the main predators.

Distribution and habitat
This fish has been introduced to Jutland, southern Finland, northeast France and Belgium. It prefers open water, over bare sand, gravel or rock.

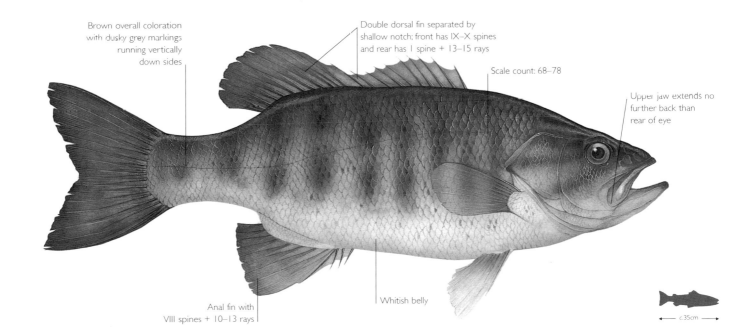

Brown overall coloration with dusky grey markings running vertically down sides

Double dorsal fin separated by shallow notch; front has IX–X spines and rear has 1 spine + 13–15 rays

Scale count: 68–78

Upper jaw extends no further back than rear of eye

Anal fin with VIII spines + 10–13 rays

Whitish belly

c.35cm

Zander *Stizostedion lucioperca*

As its alternative name of pike-perch suggests, the zander is a predator with some resemblance to two other freshwater fish. At one time it was even thought to be a hybrid of the two.

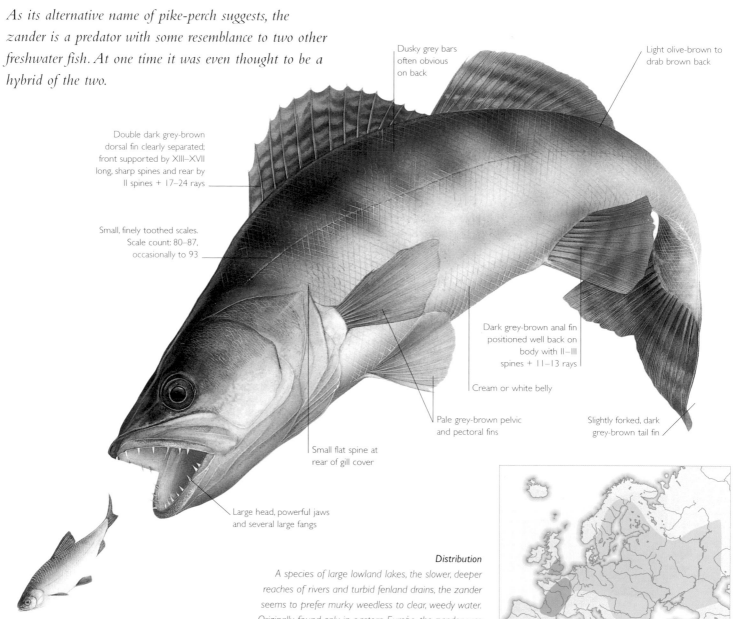

Dusky grey bars often obvious on back

Light olive-brown to drab brown back

Double dark grey-brown dorsal fin clearly separated; front supported by XIII–XVII long, sharp spines and rear by II spines + 17–24 rays

Small, finely toothed scales. Scale count: 80–87, occasionally to 93

Dark grey-brown anal fin positioned well back on body with II–III spines + 11–13 rays

Cream or white belly

Pale grey-brown pelvic and pectoral fins

Slightly forked, dark grey-brown tail fin

Small flat spine at rear of gill cover

Large head, powerful jaws and several large fangs

c.45cm+

Distribution

A species of large lowland lakes, the slower, deeper reaches of rivers and turbid fenland drains, the zander seems to prefer murky weedless to clear, weedy water. Originally found only in eastern Europe, the zander was introduced to waters in the Rhine valley, France and southeast England, from where it has spread or been introduced to other areas.

The zander has a long, torpedo-shaped body. The head is large and has powerful jaws bearing several large, curved fangs and lots of smaller teeth. There is a small, flat spine at the rear of the gill cover. The dorsal fin is double and the two parts are completely separate – the front part is supported by long, sharp spines, the second by branched rays. The tail fin is slightly forked, the anal fin is positioned well back on the tail opposite the rear dorsal (together they aid rapid acceleration), and the pelvic fins are held forwards on the body close to the pectoral fins. The scales are small and finely toothed.

General coloration varies from a light olive-brown to drab brown on the back, lightening down the sides to a cream or white belly. The zander tends to be darker in acid, peaty waters and paler in turbid water. Young and small zander often have seven to 10 dusky grey bars running down their backs as far as the lateral line. These fade as they fish age, but traces of them can often be seen high on the back. The fins are dark grey-brown, but the pectoral and pelvic fins are paler, sometimes with heavy brown-black spotting.

Breeding behaviour and life cycle

Zander spawn in April to June in water 1–3m deep. The adults congregate in suitable sites as soon as the water temperature rises above about 12°C. Weedy sites are often used, including open reed-beds. The fish do not pair; instead several males will accompany one female as she spawns.

Each female produces an equivalent of about 150,000 eggs per kilogram of her body weight. The 1.5mm-diameter, sticky, pale yellow eggs are laid among weeds, boulders or in hollows in the gravel bottom. It has been reported that both parents guard the spawning area until the eggs hatch.

Hatching occurs after seven to 10 days and the 5–6mm-long larvae feed on the remains of their yolk sacs while their fins, mouths and teeth develop. Then, as fry, they disperse and feed actively on small crustaceans and insect larvae.

Food and feeding behaviour

Zander will eat any lesser fish including small zander, carp, crucian carp, dace, roach, rudd, bitterling, minnow, bream, silver bream, bleak, gudgeon, stone loach, perch and ruffe. Maximum prey size is approximately 10 per cent of the zander's own body length. Small zander feed in loose shoals, but as they grow they become solitary feeders.

Although they will feed throughout the day, feeding intensity increases at dusk and dawn, when shoals of prey are easier to approach in the changing light. Zander also feed heavily by day in turbid water: rivers that are in spate, where a

The wide mouth of a zander is adapted for catching small fish, and its eyes for seeing small fish in the murkiest of conditions.

clay-stained stream enters a lake or where algal blooms render the lake water murky. Their eyes are specially adapted for seeing in dark or turbid conditions. Although feeding intensity declines in extremely low water temperatures, zander feed throughout the year, except during the short spawning season.

Growth and longevity

By the end of their first year, zander are about 15–20cm long, and 20–30cm at the end of the second year. Females grow more quickly than males after the first year. Males mature at two to three years, females at three to four years, when they will have attained an average length of 45cm and weight of about 1.1kg. The usual maximum length is 90cm–1.1m, weighing 5–7kg. The largest zander recorded was 12kg, 1.3m and about 20 years old.

Predators

Perch, pike and large zander are the chief fish predators and cormorants take zander from a number of lakes.

Related species
The Volga zander (Stizostedion volgensis) is a small species of zander, averaging up to 30cm long, exceptionally to 45cm, and up to 2kg. Scale counts are diagnostic and there are five to seven distinct dark grey bars extending down the sides of its body. This barring is faint and present only in smaller zander. It lives in lowland rivers and lakes that drain into the Black Sea and north Caspian Sea. Scale count: 70–79.

Conservation status of zander
Zander stocks are highly prized, but there is concern about the effects on native fish populations where it is introduced.

Asper *Zingel (Aspro) asper*

The asper is a small, zander-like fish found only in one river, the Rhone. It is very rare.

This is a very slender, streamlined fish with a slightly flattened belly. There are two well-separated dorsal fins, the first supported by spines and the second by two spines and branched rays. The anal fin is moderately based and positioned opposite the rear dorsal – both act together when the fish accelerates. The large, rounded pelvic fins are positioned well forward and their bases are beneath the pectoral fin bases.

The fins are sandy buff, the first dorsal and pectoral fins are slightly darker, and lack spotting.

Breeding behaviour and life cycle
Although this has not been studied thoroughly, it is known that the asper spawns in early spring. The eggs are 1–1.5mm in diameter, pale yellow and laid among stones in shallow, slow-flowing water. It is not known whether the females deliberately bury their eggs in a stone nest or whether the eggs are washed into cavities under stones. The incubation period is probably one to two weeks. It has been reported that the fry feed in open water before adopting an adult lifestyle on the bottom.

Food and feeding behaviour
By day the asper lives on the bottom of deep pools; at night it moves into shallower, fast-flowing water in pool necks and riffles to feed. Mayfly nymphs, caddis and midge larvae, freshwater shrimps and aquatic snails are abundant in the parts of the river system where it lives and these probably dominate its diet.

Growth and longevity
Little information is available, but two adults measured 13.5 and 14.5cm. The age of maturity unknown, but is probably two years.

Predators
Nobody knows what eats the asper, but fry predators probably include large trout and chub, and grey herons take adults when they move into shallow water at dusk.

Distribution and habitat
The asper is found only in the upper and middle reaches of the River Rhone system.

Conservation status of asper
Since the construction of many dams and the canalisation of some lengths of the river, this fish has become very rare and must be considered an endangered species.

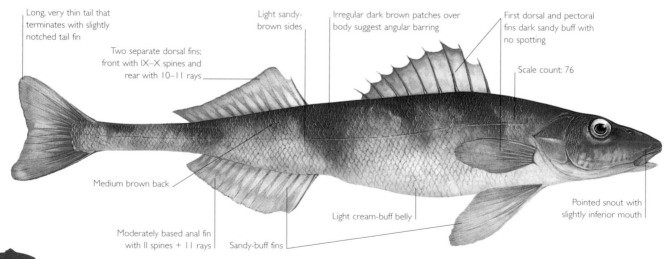

Long, very thin tail that terminates with slightly notched tail fin

Two separate dorsal fins; front with IX–X spines and rear with 10–11 rays

Light sandy-brown sides

Irregular dark brown patches over body suggest angular barring

First dorsal and pectoral fins dark sandy buff with no spotting

Scale count: 76

Medium brown back

Moderately based anal fin with 11 spines + 11 rays

Sandy-buff fins

Light cream-buff belly

Pointed snout with slightly inferior mouth

c.14cm

Asprete
Romanichthys valsanicola

This small, slender fish is Europe's most recently discovered fish and is now one of the rarest.

The asprete is a long, slender fish which looks rather like a hybrid between a miller's thumb and a ruffe. The body is at its broadest and flattened along the back, but it tapers quickly behind the vent, along the tail, where it is rounded. There are two dorsal fins separated by a short, but distinct bar; the first dorsal is supported by spines, the second by branched rays. The anal fin is fairly short-based and lies opposite the rear dorsal. The tail fin is slightly notched and the pelvic fins are positioned well forward with their bases beneath the pectoral fin bases.

Breeding behaviour and life cycle

The breeding behaviour of the very rare asprete has never been studied, which begs the question: how can we conserve such rare a species if we know so little about it?

Food and feeding behaviour

The asprete hides away under boulders during the day and it appears to be a nocturnal feeder. It is very sensitive to light. The foods available to the asprete are the invertebrates of a typical mountain stream: stonefly and mayfly nymphs predominate, with some two-winged fly larvae (torrent-midges) and a few caddis. Two aspretes took chopped up earthworms drifted down to them, which suggests they are opportunistic feeders. Little else is known about their feeding habits.

Growth and longevity

This has not been studied, but the average length of five specimens examined in 1989 was 9.1cm (range 8–11cm). Maximum size is considered to be about 13cm.

Predators

There are few predators of aspretes, but miller's thumbs might take eggs or larvae.

Distribution and habitat

The asprete was discovered in 1957 living in boulder-strewn, fast water and turbulent lengths of three tributaries of the River Arges in Romania: the Argesul, the Riul Doamnei and the Vislan.

Conservation status of asprete

When it was first discovered this fish appeared to be quite numerous, but it has not been recorded from the Argesul or Riul Doamnei for some years, and it has become rare in the Vislan. The cause of this demise is development in these upland valleys, which has involved silting the boulder reaches and pesticide pollution. The asprete is now endangered.

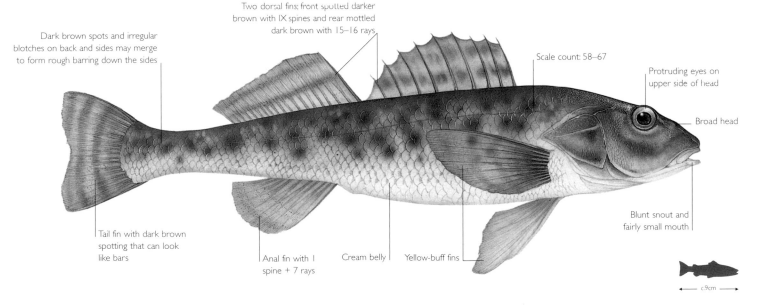

Two dorsal fins; front spotted darker brown with IX spines and rear mottled dark brown with 15–16 rays

Dark brown spots and irregular blotches on back and sides may merge to form rough barring down the sides

Scale count: 58–67

Protruding eyes on upper side of head

Broad head

Tail fin with dark brown spotting that can look like bars

Anal fin with 1 spine + 7 rays

Cream belly

Yellow-buff fins

Blunt snout and fairly small mouth

c.9cm

Streber *Zingel (Aspro) streber*

The streber is a very rare, small nocturnal fish, which is closely related to the asper. It occurs in the Danube river system.

This is a small, very slender, spindle-like fish. The head is broad on top, but it tapers from the side to a pointed snout. There are two well-separated dorsal fins, the first supported by sharp spines, the second by branched rays. The anal fin is opposite the rear dorsal; the large, rounded pelvic fins are held forward, beneath the pectoral fins.

Breeding behaviour and life cycle
The streber spawns in March and April in shallow, gravel- or shingle-bottomed riffles or pool necks where the flow is steady and moderately fast. They spawn at night, each female shedding about 3000, 1.5mm-diameter, pale yellow eggs among stones. These hatch after about 10 days and the larvae remain close by until they have grown to about 2.5cm when they move into deeper water.

Food and feeding behaviour
Although it is not a shoal species, the streber does associate loosely with others especially in the day, when it seeks deep, dark pools. At dusk the streber moves into shallower, turbulent water where it feeds on invertebrates on the river bed. Stonefly and mayfly nymphs, caddis larvae and freshwater shrimps dominate the diet, although it will also feed on the eggs and tiny fry of other fish species.

Growth and longevity
Most adult streber are 12–18cm (mean of 14, 15.5cm) long and there are reports of specimens of 22cm. They probably mature at two years old and have lived for a maximum of four to five years.

Predators
In the small rivers inhabited by streber, grey herons are probably the main predator of adults, while large brown and rainbow trout probably devour many fry.

Distribution and habitat
The streber is a species that is found in small streams and mountain brooks throughout the Danube catchment. It has also been recorded in mountain streams in Bulgaria.

Conservation status of streber
This is not a common fish and it is found in small groups wherever there are deep pools with gravel riffles in small streams. In recent years the populations appear to have declined to the point where it must be considered an endangered species.

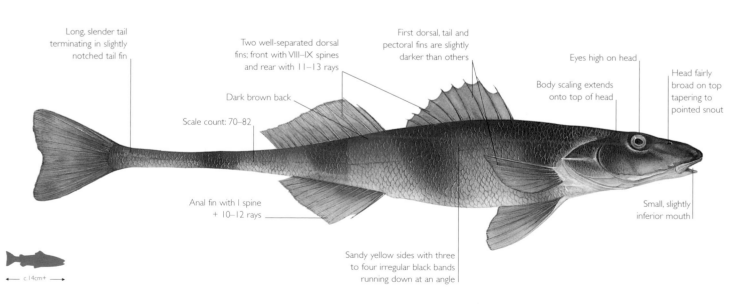

Long, slender tail terminating in slightly notched tail fin

Two well-separated dorsal fins; front with VIII–IX spines and rear with 11–13 rays

First dorsal, tail and pectoral fins are slightly darker than others

Eyes high on head

Dark brown back

Body scaling extends onto top of head

Head fairly broad on top tapering to pointed snout

Scale count: 70–82

Anal fin with I spine + 10–12 rays

Sandy yellow sides with three to four irregular black bands running down at an angle

Small, slightly inferior mouth

c 14cm+

Zingel *Zingel (Aspro) zingel*

This member of the perch family lives in only two rivers and little is known about its natural history.

The zingel is a long, slender, streamlined little fish. Scales extend from the body onto the top of the head. There are two dorsal fins with a clear gap between them that is not as great as in other Zingel species. The large pelvic fins are carried forward on the body and their bases are slightly behind those of the pectoral fins; the anal fin is set opposite the rear dorsal fin. The fins are all buff and unspotted, but the first dorsal and tail fins are usually darker than the others.

Breeding behaviour and life cycle

The zingel spawns at night in March to April in gravel- or shingle-bottomed, fairly shallow, fast riffles. Each female produces approximately 5000, 1.5mm-diameter, pale yellow eggs that are hidden under stones. The incubation period is unknown, but is probably one to two weeks.

Food and feeding behaviour

A bottom-feeder, the zingel spends the day hiding under boulders or among roots in the river bank, emerging at night to feed. Little detailed information is available about what the zingel eats, but its diet probably includes large invertebrates that live on the river bed: stonefly and mayfly nymphs, caddis larvae, freshwater shrimps, snails and the eggs and small fry of other fish.

Growth and longevity

The zingel is larger than other *Zingel* species, with a mean length of 17.75cm (range 15–22cm) in a sample of 18. Some have grown to 35–40cm. It probably matures at two to three years. Longevity is probably no more than five years.

Predators

Unknown, but adults are probably eaten by pike, grey herons and perhaps cormorants.

Distribution and habitat

The zingel is found in the middle reaches of the Danube and Dniester Rivers, where the flow is fast and there are deep pools and plenty of adjacent, shallower riffles. It avoids sluggish, mud- or silt-bottomed reaches.

Conservation status of zingel

River damming and agricultural pollution, perhaps mainly by pesticides, has greatly reduced zingel populations to the point where this species must be considered endangered.

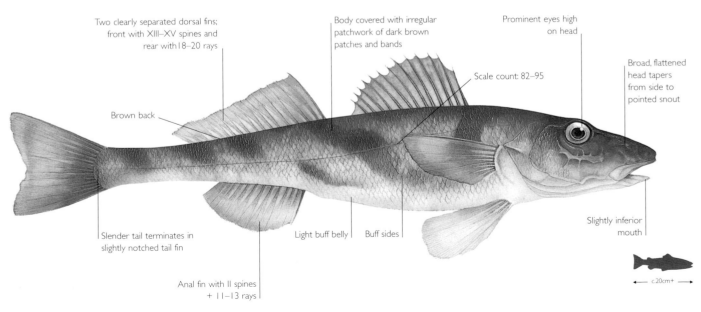

Two clearly separated dorsal fins; front with XIII–XV spines and rear with 18–20 rays

Body covered with irregular patchwork of dark brown patches and bands

Prominent eyes high on head

Scale count: 82–95

Broad, flattened head tapers from side to pointed snout

Brown back

Slender tail terminates in slightly notched tail fin

Light buff belly

Buff sides

Slightly inferior mouth

Anal fin with II spines + 11–13 rays

c.20cm+

Thick-lipped Mullet *Chelon labrosus*

Mullets are marine fish that move into estuaries to feed in summer, often penetrating fresh water. They are quite large fish, yet they take the tiniest of foodstuffs.

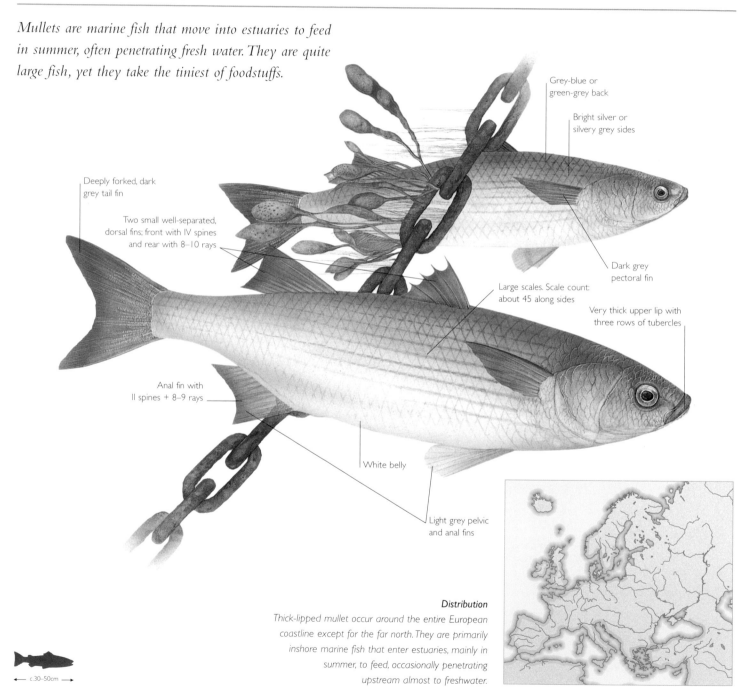

Grey-blue or green-grey back

Bright silver or silvery grey sides

Deeply forked, dark grey tail fin

Two small well-separated, dorsal fins; front with IV spines and rear with 8–10 rays

Dark grey pectoral fin

Large scales. Scale count: about 45 along sides

Very thick upper lip with three rows of tubercles

Anal fin with II spines + 8–9 rays

White belly

Light grey pelvic and anal fins

c. 30–50cm

Distribution
Thick-lipped mullet occur around the entire European coastline except for the far north. They are primarily inshore marine fish that enter estuaries, mainly in summer, to feed, occasionally penetrating upstream almost to freshwater.

All mullets can be identified by their streamlined, but sturdy body covered with large scales that extend on the top of the broad head to just in front of the eye. There is no lateral line. There are two well-separated, small dorsal fins (the first supported by spines, the second by branched rays); the pelvic fins are carried well forward on the body; the tail fin is moderately, deeply forked.

The upper lip is very thick (the depth is about 10 per cent of head length) and it has two to three rows of conspicuous, short, bristle-like tubercles. There is a narrow band of transparent fatty material around the edges of the eyes.

The back is grey-blue or green-grey, the sides are bright silver or silvery grey and the belly is white. The pectoral, dorsal and tail fins are dark grey, the pelvic and anal fins are a lighter grey.

Breeding behaviour and life cycle

Thick-lipped mullet spawn in shallow, inshore waters. In the Mediterranean spawning occurs at the coolest time of the year, January to March; around the Iberian coastline, late January to April; and around the shores of northwest Europe when sea termperatures are at their highest, late June to early September.

Thick-lipped mullet are shoal spawners, each female shedding huge numbers of 1mm-diameter, clear eggs, which are fertilised by the males shedding sperm. The eggs from one female will probably, therefore, be fertilised by several males, while one male will fertilise eggs from several females. Small females may produce less than one million eggs, although most produce far more: a 42cm female had about 4.8 million, and a 49cm female 5.2 million.

The eggs are pelagic, floating passively with the currents until they hatch, presumably after a very few days. The fry then move to the sea bed, head inshore to shallower waters and commence feeding on microscopic algae.

Food and feeding behaviour

Thick-lipped mullet browse rock or mud surfaces and devour diatoms, fine seaweed and microscopic crustaceans (ostracods and copepods), or they ingest large amounts of mud and extract small invertebrates, such as tiny worms, snails and crustaceans, and algae. One angler watched mullets in an estuary taking tiny pieces of the green alga *Enteromorpha* floating downstream. He tied some green mohair to a hook and caught a 2.3kg fish.

The fact that mullets take such tiny foods, which cannot usually be used as baits, has always frustrated anglers. However, they have exploited the fact that mullets will take just about any soft, fragile organic matter by using bread as bait. Indeed, thick-lipped mullet find white bread so much to their liking that shoals will stop feeding on natural foods when bread is thrown onto the water and will rise to the surface and batter large pieces, taking the soggy crumbs as they sink.

Thick-lipped mullet are shoal fish, moving inshore with the flooding tide and out on the ebb, with their dorsal fins showing, often immediately behind the advancing water. Although they feed inshore throughout the year in the Mediterranean, in northwest Europe they move into estuaries as the water warms in late spring, from mid-May, and head south or into deeper water in autumn.

Growth and longevity

Thick-lipped mullet grow to approximately 10–15cm after one year, about 20–25cm after two years and 25–30cm after three years when a

Mullets are one of the most abundant inshore and estuary fish. They will eat just about any organic matter and anglers can attract them with bread!

proportion of that age class mature. The normal maximum length is approximately 50cm, exceptionally 75cm, weighing up to 4.5kg. Thick-lipped mullet are long-lived fish, and usually live for at least 10 years, and have been known to survive for 20 years or more.

Predators

The fry are food for the full range of inshore predators of small fish, including birds such as terns and red-breasted mergansers, and fish such as sea bass and sea trout. Larger thick-lipped mullet may feature in the diets of harbour seals and cormorants when they are in estuaries.

> **Conservation status of thick-lipped mullet**
> This is an abundant species, which is an important seafood for humans, especially in the Mediterranean and around the coast of Spain and Portugal. It is not easy to catch in a net by day, for it will leap over the net to avoid capture, and is best netted at night.

Thin-lipped Mullet *Liza ramada*

Although it is a marine fish, the thin-lipped mullet is a common estuary species throughout most of Europe, often penetrating freshwater completely.

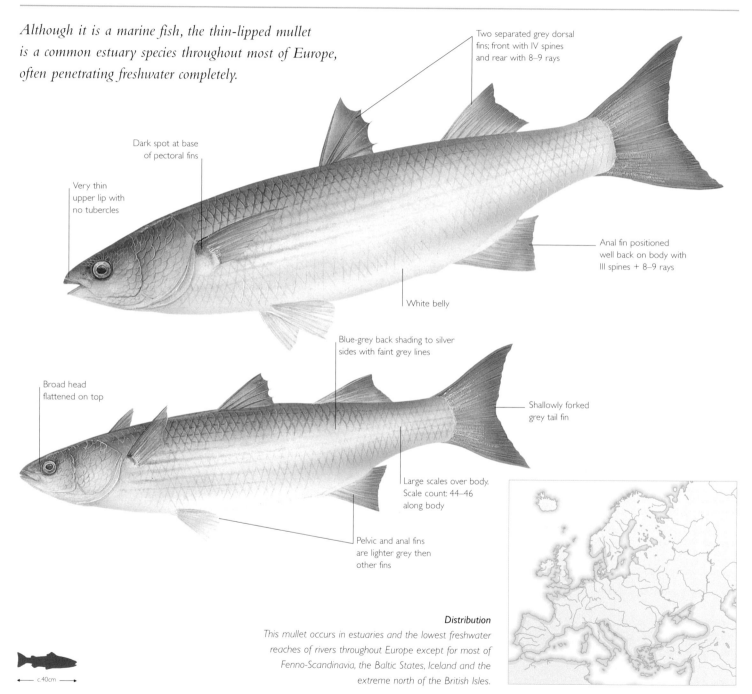

Two separated grey dorsal fins; front with IV spines and rear with 8–9 rays

Dark spot at base of pectoral fins

Very thin upper lip with no tubercles

Anal fin positioned well back on body with III spines + 8–9 rays

White belly

Blue-grey back shading to silver sides with faint grey lines

Broad head flattened on top

Shallowly forked grey tail fin

Large scales over body. Scale count: 44–46 along body

Pelvic and anal fins are lighter grey then other fins

c.40cm

Distribution

This mullet occurs in estuaries and the lowest freshwater reaches of rivers throughout Europe except for most of Fenno-Scandinavia, the Baltic States, Iceland and the extreme north of the British Isles.

The thin-lipped mullet has a streamlined body with sturdy shoulders and a broad head that is flattened on top. The upper lip is very thin and has no tubercles. There is a narrow band of transparent fatty material around the edges of the eyes. Large scales extend over the body onto the top of the head and forward to the nostrils. There are two well-separated, small dorsal fins, the first supported by spines, the second by rays. The anal fin is positioned well back on the body opposite the rear dorsal so both fins can be used together; the tail fin is shallowly forked.

Coloration is basically silvery; the blue-grey back shades to silver sides along which are faint grey lines and the belly is white. There is a distinct dark spot at the base of the pectoral fins. All the fins are grey, but the pelvic and anal fins are much lighter than the pectoral, dorsal and tail fins.

Breeding behaviour and life cycle

Relatively little is known about the breeding behaviour of thin-lipped mullet, despite the fact that they are widespread and common. They do spawn communally in inshore waters during the summer and huge numbers of 1mm-diameter eggs are produced. The eggs drift pelagically as part of the zooplankton for the few days before they hatch and the young are probably pelagic for the first few days of life.

Food and feeding behaviour

Thin-lipped mullet are shoal fish and primarily eat algae, which they browse from mudflats and rocks. In calm conditions, you can deduce the location of feeding mullet on mudflats by the marks made in the mud surface by grazing fish.

Stomach analyses of thin-lipped mullet often reveal the presence of very tiny invertebrates, such as crustaceans, molluscs and polychaete worms, which were probably ingested inadvertently with algae. Mullets will also devour some quite fetid foods. For instance, there is, below the lighthouse on Europa Point at the southern tip of the Rock of Gibraltar, a sewage outfall that pumps a stream of raw sewage soup out into the Mediterranean. On either side of this band are huge shoals of mullets, totalling many

thousands, tightly packed, the fish jostling for position with lips at the surface as they suck down the soup. Mullets have also been recorded sucking the rotting corpse of a sheep that had been washed into the shallow water of an estuary.

Mullets love bread and a shoal will rapidly be attracted to pieces thrown onto the water (see Bread and fish below). They locate these unnatural types of food by their sense of taste. There have been observations of mullet homing in on water in which bread has been soaked.

Thin-lipped mullet generally feed with the tide, following it up the shore and retreating before the ebb, although in areas with a small tidal range they may feed in harbours and marinas throughout the day.

Growth and longevity

This has not been well studied, but it is known that most grow to about 40cm in length or 1.5kg in weight, with exceptional specimens exceeding 50cm and 2.5kg.

Predators

While fry are prey for a host of bird, such as divers, grebes, terns, mergansers and herons, and fish predators, the cormorant and harbour seal are probably the major predators of adults; perhaps also grey herons in shallow estuaries. Numbers of gannets from the Atlantic and the small resident Gibraltar population of shags feed on the sewage-eating mullet of Europa Point. Despite being very palatable and appearing on large fish markets, mullets are not popular food for humans.

Bread and fish

If you want to know whether there are mullets about, throw a big slice of white bread into the water. Mullet shoals will home in on the floating bread and you will see them sucking particles from it. Many forms of wildlife find white bread attractive. I have recorded 61 species of wild European bird eating bread. Most land mammals love bread (including badgers who prefer it buttered). And it is the most outstanding bait for many European freshwater fish.

Related species

The golden mullet (Liza aurata) has a thin upper lip and there are no tubercles. There is a very narrow band of transparent fatty material around the edges of the eyes. Scales on top of the head extend forward to the nostrils. The body is tinged with yellow and there are distinct yellow spots on each gill cover and immediately behind the eye. It occurs in inshore waters from the British Isles and Denmark southwards.

The sharp-nosed mullet (Liza saliens) again has no tubercles on its upper lip, but there is no band of transparent fatty material around the edges of the eyes. Scales on top of the head extend forward to just in front of the eye. The body has a slight yellow cast and there are several tiny yellow spots on the gill cover. The sharp-nosed mullet occurs from the Bay of Biscay south and throughout the Mediterranean and Black Sea.

The striped mullet (Mugil cephalus) has a thin upper lip and lacks tubercles. The eyes are covered with transparent fatty material to the pupils. Scales on top of the head are very tiny and extend forward to the end of the snout. The body has a slight buff tinge. This species occurs from the Bay of Biscay south (with records from southwest England), through the Mediterranean and Black Seas, to the coast of west Africa; it often occurs in the lower reaches of rivers.

The smooth-lipped mullet (Oedalechilus labeo) has a very thick upper lip (as great as eye diameter), which lacks tubercles. It also lacks fatty tissue around the eyes. Scales on top of the head do not reach forward as far as the eyes. This is entirely a Mediterranean species and rarely enters brackish water.

Conservation status of thin-lipped mullet
This species is a very common and often abundant fish. Most estuaries within its range have huge shoals.

Freshwater Blenny *Blennius fluviatilis*

Blennies are well-known inhabitants of saltwater rock pools around western and southern European coasts. Only one species is found in freshwater.

The freshwater blenny is a small, scaleless, slimy fish. Its head is short, but conspicuous, especially in males, as it appears to bulge out of the front of the body. The body is flattened on the belly and widest behind the pectoral fin bases, tapering slowly to the vent and along the tail. The pelvic fins are reduced to two long rays positioned at the extreme front of the body. These are used by the fish to lift its head up off the bottom. The fins have a light-brown background colour, but the dorsal and tail fins have darker banding.

Breeding behaviour and life cycle

Freshwater blennies spawn from April to July in areas. The 1mm-diameter eggs are laid in cavities under stones and are guarded by the male who fans them with his pectoral fins to keep them supplied with oxygenated water. One male might guard the eggs of more than one female or one female may produce several batches of eggs in the male's nest. The incubation period is probably four to five weeks. After leaving the nest initially the 4–5mm larvae probably feed on zooplankton.

Food and feeding behaviour

The freshwater blenny feeds on the river or lake bed watching out for suitable prey by perching on top of a rock and propping its head up with its pelvic fins. Invertebrates form the bulk of its diet, but it will eat eggs and fry of other fish.

Growth and longevity

Further study is required, but adults grow to about 8cm, exceptionally 15cm. Nobody knows when it matures, but it is probably at one to two years. It is likely to live for a maximum of five years.

Predators

The freshwater blenny's predators probably include several species of herons, such as night and squacco herons, and little bitterns.

Distribution and habitat

The freshwater blenny occurs from southern Spain east through Turkey and Cyprus. It occurs in clearwater, brackish lagoons, slow rivers and freshwater lakes.

Conservation status of freshwater blenny
This species is common in many areas, but some populations have suffered through drainage and pollution of its lowland waters.

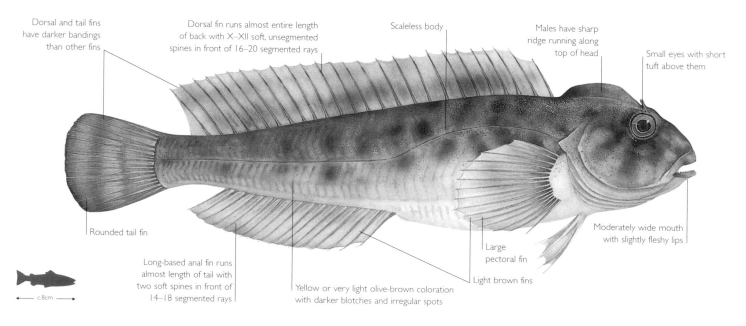

Dorsal and tail fins have darker bandings than other fins

Dorsal fin runs almost entire length of back with X–XII soft, unsegmented spines in front of 16–20 segmented rays

Scaleless body

Males have sharp ridge running along top of head

Small eyes with short tuft above them

Rounded tail fin

Long-based anal fin runs almost length of tail with two soft spines in front of 14–18 segmented rays

Yellow or very light olive-brown coloration with darker blotches and irregular spots

Large pectoral fin

Light brown fins

Moderately wide mouth with slightly fleshy lips

c.8cm

Common Goby *Pomatoschistus microps*

This is the most widespread and abundant of the several species of gobies that occur throughout Europe in fresh or slightly brackish water.

The common goby is a small, stoutly built fish. It has two separated dorsal fins, the first supported by soft spines, the second by rays. The anal fin is opposite the second dorsal fin. The pectoral fins are large and rounded; the pelvic fins are joined together and flattened to form a sucker-disc that, although weak, helps the fish fix itself onto a rock.

Breeding behaviour and life cycle

As the sea warms in spring, common gobies move to shallow water where they spend the summer feeding and breeding. Each female produces several batches of eggs in the spawning season, which lasts from April to the end of August or early September. The fish pair and the female sheds a batch of 1mm-long oval eggs inside the empty shell of a cockle, clam or mussel, which the male guards until hatching occurs after seven to 10 days. The larvae disperse and grow quickly on a diet of microscopic plankton. Each female produces around 3000–4000 eggs and by October the population may be huge. As the sea temperature falls, the fish move offshore into deep water.

Food and feeding behaviour

In estuaries, the diet of the common goby is dominated by small crustaceans. In brackish water, midge larvae and pupae, and crustaceans are the chief foods. They also eat zooplankton, including the larvae of crabs and other crustaceans.

Growth and longevity

Females are slightly larger than males of the same age, and they have an average length of 5–6cm. They probably spawn at two years old and live for no more than four to five years.

Predators

A major food of herons, terns and mergansers in some clear water estuaries, common gobies also feature in the diet of bass and sea trout.

Distribution and habitat

This fish occurs in coastal waters, estuaries and brackish pools from south Norway and the southern Baltic, south and west around the British Isles and Iberian Peninsula to Gibraltar.

Conservation status of common goby
This species is common and often abundant throughout its range.

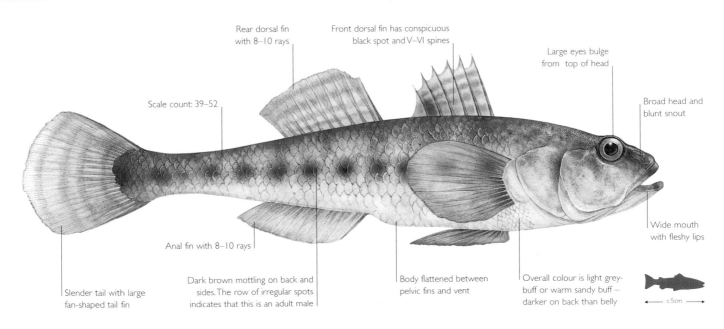

Rear dorsal fin with 8–10 rays

Front dorsal fin has conspicuous black spot and V–VI spines

Large eyes bulge from top of head

Scale count: 39–52

Broad head and blunt snout

Anal fin with 8–10 rays

Wide mouth with fleshy lips

Slender tail with large fan-shaped tail fin

Dark brown mottling on back and sides. The row of irregular spots indicates that this is an adult male

Body flattened between pelvic fins and vent

Overall colour is light grey-buff or warm sandy buff – darker on back than belly

c.5cm

Mediterranean and Black Sea Gobies

These gobies are found in brackish and freshwater habitats around the Mediterranean and Black Seas. Identification can be difficult and is not helped by taxonomists who attempt to split single species into two or more on seemingly fairly minor grounds.

General goby identification

The broad head has a blunt or fairly blunt snout and rounded cheeks. The wide mouth has thick, or fairly thick, fleshy lips; the eyes are on the top of the head. The body is cylindrical and usually flattened underneath, and the tail tapers; the body may be fully scaled or naked. There are two dorsal fins, the first with soft spines, the second with rays. The anal fin is opposite the second dorsal. The pectoral fins are large and round. The pelvic fins are joined together and flattened to form a sucker disc. The overall coloration of the head, body and fins is some shade of light brown and there are usually darker brown markings.

All gobies are bottom-dwelling fish and, in most cases, their natural history is not thoroughly known. Use the following features, including the location in which you find your fish, to complete identification.

Canestrini's goby *(Potamoschistus canestrinii)*

The back is scaleless from the rear of the second dorsal fin to the head and the front of the belly is also scaleless. The maximum length is about 5–6cm in males and 6–6.5cm in females. The Canestrini's goby occurs in estuaries and brackish lagoons from the Po delta east to northern Dalmatia. Although it is still locally common, industrial pollution and the development of coastal habitats in this region have destroyed several populations, making it endangered.

Ray count: rear dorsal fin 8–9
Scale count: 36–42

Orsini's goby *(Knipowitschia punctatissima)*

The body is naked except for a small patch of scales behind the pectoral fins. The maximum length of an Orsino's goby is about 5cm. This is an entirely freshwater species found in slow-flowing streams in northern Italy where it is common. It has also been described in the Matica River, Croatia.

Ray count: rear dorsal fin 7–8

Marten's goby *(Padogobius martensii)*

This goby has no scales on the nape or head. Maximum length is 8.5cm. The Marten's goby lives only in freshwater in stony rivers, such as Po,

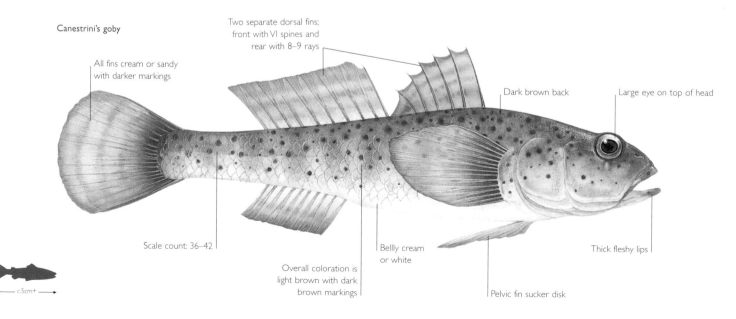

Canestrini's goby

Two separate dorsal fins; front with VI spines and rear with 8–9 rays

All fins cream or sandy with darker markings

Dark brown back

Large eye on top of head

Scale count: 36–42

Bellly cream or white

Overall coloration is light brown with dark brown markings

Pelvic fin sucker disk

Thick fleshy lips

c.5cm+

Adige, Brenta and Soca, flowing into the northern shore of the Adriatic and some clean lakes. It is a relatively common fish.

Ray count: rear dorsal fin 9–11
Scale count: 29–44

Arno goby (Padogobius nigricans)

There are no scales on the nape or head of the Arno goby and the maximum length is about 12cm. Very closely related to the Marten's goby, this species occurs only in freshwater habitats, stone-bottomed streamy streams and lake margins, in the northern Apennines of Italy immediately south of the range of Marten's goby. It is fairly common.

Ray count: rear dorsal fin 11–12
Scale count: 40–50

Monkey goby (Neogobius fluviatilis)

Scales cover the nape and the maximum length is 18–20cm. It occurs in freshwater (rivers and lakes up to 400km from the sea), estuaries and brackish water around the Black and Caspian Seas. Once common, this species is now declining and perhaps endangered.

Ray count: rear dorsal fin 14–17
Scale count: 55–61

Round goby (Neogobius melanostomus)

Scales cover the nape and the maximum length is 20–22.5cm. This goby occurs in the Black Sea and enters estuaries and other slightly brackish habitats. It is abundant.

Ray count: rear dorsal fin 15–16
Scale count: 45–57

Black Sea goby (Proterorhinus marmoratus)

Scales cover the nape and the nostrils are unique: they extend forward as a tube. The maximum length is 10cm. This species lives in rivers draining into the Black and Caspian Seas. It is still locally common, but pollution and the drying up or drainage of some rivers have made it very rare in some parts of its range. This goby should be considered endangered.

Ray count: rear dorsal fin 15–16
Scale count: 42–50

Knout goby (Mesogobius batrachocephalus)

Scales cover the nape of the Knout goby and the maximum length is approximately 30–5cm. The knout goby is Europe's largest goby and it occurs around the Black Sea. It is common, but is rarely found in freshwater.

Ray count: rear dorsal fin 16–19
Scale count: 75–82

Tadpole goby (Benthophilus stellatus)

This goby is scaleless, but there are rows of spiny plates running down its thin, tapering body. The first dorsal fin extremely small. It grows to a maximum length of 10–12.5cm. This goby occurs in the lower reaches of rivers and in estuaries draining into the north of the Black Sea and into the Caspian Sea. Some scientists have split this into several species. Many populations have been lost due to pollution and, although it is still locally common, the tadpole goby should be considered an endangered species.

Ray count: rear dorsal fin 7–8

Caucasian goby (Knipowitschia caucasica)

The head and the back in front of the first dorsal fin are scaleless. This goby grows to a maximum length of 4–5cm. It lives around the shores of the Black Sea and can tolerate a wide range of salinities from pure freshwater through full strength seawater to higher concentrations in coastal lagoons. The Caucasian goby is abundant, although many freshwater populations have declined through pollution and the drying up of its natural habitats.

Ray count: rear dorsal fin 8–9
Scale count: 31–38

Lesser Black Sea goby (Knipowitschia longecaudata)

The head and back in front of the front of the second dorsal fin are scaleless. The lesser Black Sea goby grows to a maximum length of 4cm. Found in fresh and brackish water around the Black and Caspian Seas, this species is locally common, but has suffered from pollution and the draining and drying up of its habitat in places.

Ray count: rear dorsal fin 7–8
Scale count: 33–35

Verga's goby (Knipowitschia panizzae)

The head and back in front of the second dorsal fin are scaleless and its maximum length is approximately 4cm. This small goby is found in brackish lagoons around the Adriatic, and in freshwater lakes and rivers in northern Italy. It is locally common, but some populations have been lost through pollution and industrial development of coastal sites.

Ray count: rear dorsal fin 8–9
Scale count: 31–39

Pinios goby (Knipowitschia thessala)

This goby's body is naked except for a patch of scales behind its pectoral fins and the midline of the tail. It grows to a maximum length of approximately 4cm. An entirely freshwater species, the Pinios goby is found only in the Pinios River and its tributaries in Greece. It should be considered an endangered species.

Ray count: rear dorsal fin 6–7

Pygmy goby (Economidichthys pygmaeus)

The belly and back from the middle of the second dorsal fin are scaleless. The area in front of the vent is a swollen and pitted organ. This goby grows to a maximum length of approximately 5cm. It is a freshwater species that is found only in the Greek rivers Arkathos, Louros and Vlyho, and in Lake Trikhonis. Its river populations are probably endangered because of pollution and habitat damage.

Ray count: rear dorsal fin 8–9
Scale count: 30–38

Dwarf goby (Economidichthys trichonis)

Its body is naked except for a patch of scales below the first dorsal fin and along the midline of the tail. It has a small swollen and pitted organ in front of the vent. The maximum length is approximately 3cm in males, but less than 2cm in females. This is Europe's smallest freshwater fish and it occurs only in the upper reaches of River Akheloos and its Lake Trikhonis. It is of such local distribution that it must be considered an endangered species.

Ray count: rear dorsal fin 10–11

Flounder _Platichthys flesus_

Flatfish are predominantly species of shallow sandy or gravel-bottomed inshore seas. The flounder is an exception for, although it spends most of its life in brackish estuaries and bays, it commonly penetrates freshwater.

Straight lateral line over most of body, curving upwards slightly close to gill cover

Eyes are usually on right-hand side of body

Eyeless side is white, sometimes with pale buff blotching

Dorsal fin with 52–67 rays has sharp, bony spines along base

Scale count: 80–90

Dull grey-brown or dark grey-olive on eyed side, with dull reddish or orange-yellow blotches and darker mottling (fins are similarly marked)

Anal fin with 35–46 rays has sharp, bony spines along base

c.30cm+

Distribution
Widespread along the entire coastline of Europe except for Iceland, the flounder occurs in all clean estuaries and upstream into the lower freshwater reaches.

The flounder body is typical of flatfish: it is laterally flattened and rounded, with both eyes and dark skin pigmentation usually on the right-hand side of the body. Its dorsal fin extends from the head to just before the tail fin, and the anal fin is about two-thirds the length of the dorsal fin; both fins have sharp, bony spines along their bases.

Breeding behaviour and life cycle

In mid- to late winter, flounders migrate from estuaries and bays to the open sea to spawn. The 1mm eggs are laid from March to May on the bottom at depths to 40m, but after they have been fertilised, they float to the surface and drift with the currents. Each female produces between 500,000 and two million eggs, depending on her size and, as spawning is a communal affair, the eggs of one female may be fertilised by sperm from several males. Where flounders and plaice spawn in close proximity, hybrids have resulted. After spawning is over, the adults return quickly to their inshore feeding grounds.

The eggs hatch after five to 10 days at sea temperatures of 8–12°C. The larvae are 3mm long, transparent, symmetrical, rounded fish and are pelagic. After their yolk sacs have been absorbed after two to three days, the larvae feed on planktonic crustaceans. In June to July, when they have grown to about 10–20mm, the fry

move inshore to shallow water and begin to metamorphose to the flatfish form. One eye, usually the left one, migrates to the other side of the head, the body flattens laterally, the side with eyes becomes pigmented, and the flounder settles on the sea bed. Many enter estuaries and a large proportion may pass upstream into freshwater.

Food and feeding behaviour

In the freshwater of rivers, flounders feed on tiny invertebrates found in the sand or silt of the river bed. In two rivers in northern England, midge larvae and pupae, caddis larvae and aquatic snails feature heavily in the diet, although during a spate they also eat earthworms, slugs and *tipulid* larvae that have been washed from fields.

In estuaries and inshore waters, marine worms, including *Arenicola* and *Nereis* species, bivalve molluscs, such as *Macoma*, and crustaceans, especially shore-crab and shrimps, are major foods. They also take small fish.

Flounders are predominantly nocturnal feeders, but they will feed during the day in rivers when the water is coloured after heavy rain. In estuaries they will also feed keenly on daytime tides. When not feeding actively, flounders burrow in sand and mud with just their eyes showing. Should shrimps or small fry swim too close, they move forwards quickly to suck them into their mouths.

Flounders are the only flatfish that are able to survive in pure freshwater.

Growth and longevity

At one year the flounder is about 10cm in length, at two years up to 15cm. Few live for more than five years, when they measure 30cm in length and weigh 800–1200g. Flounders mature at two to three years (males one year before the females).

Predators

The flounder is a most important food source for fish-eating birds, especially the cormorant. After their breeding season, European ospreys often feed on flounders in estuaries prior to their long autumn migration to West Africa. Herons and harbour seals also predate larger flounders. Red-breasted mergansers, gulls and terns take flounder fry that have recently entered shallow water.

Related species
The arctic flounder (Liopsetta glacialis) replaces the flounder from Norway's north cape eastwards along the shores of the Arctic Ocean. Like the flounder it is frequently found in estuaries and it sometimes penetrates upstream into freshwater. The arctic flounder is most easily identified by the bold black spotting that it has on the dark brown (pigmented) side of its body.

Conservation status of flounder
Although common in clean estuaries, where it also may enter freshwater, this species is absent from many estuaries because of pollution. It is delicious to eat, especially when freshly caught, but the nature of its estuary habitat makes it difficult to catch in commercial quantities. It is caught commercially in the Baltic, however. Because of their importance in estuary ecosystems, flounder populations should be carefully monitored and excessive exploitation resisted.

Glossary

References in CAPITALS are to other entries within the glossary.

Adipose fin A soft, fleshy fin located on the back of a fish, behind the DORSAL FIN. It is found in certain species, including all members of the salmon family. See page 20 for fish structure.

Aestivate To spend the summer sleeping or in a state of suspended animation.

Alevin A LARVA of trout or salmon.

Anadromous A fish that spawns in freshwater, but migrates to sea to feed and grow, such as the salmon.

Anal fin The unpaired fin located on the underside of a fish, behind the vent.

Ammocoetes The immature stage in the life cycle of lampreys.

Barbel A slender, often sensitive, outgrowth or 'feeler' found near the mouth of bottom-feeding fish, such as barbels, gudgeons and loaches.

Benthic This describes creatures living at the bottom of lakes or rivers.

Blackfly Aquatic insects in the genus *Simulium* that are a major source of food for insect-eating river fish.

Bloodworm Bright red LARVAE of some of the midge family that are favourite foods amongst bottom-dwelling lake fish.

Catadromous Fish that spawn in the sea but enter freshwater to feed, such as the eel.

Cladoceran Member of a planktonic group of crustaceans that grow to about 3mm in length. *Daphnia* is the best known species of this group.

Copepod Member of a planktonic group of crustaceans that grow to about 2mm in length. *Cyclops* is the best known species of this group.

Crepuscular Fish that are most active around dusk and dawn.

Cusp A point on a tooth that may be pointed or rounded. It is important in lamprey identification.

Cyprinid The umbrella name for all members of the carp family (*Cyprinidae*).

Diurnal Fish that are most active by day.

Dorsal fin The fin on the back of a fish that can be either double or single. See page 20 for fish structure.

Endangered A word to describe a fish that is either on the verge of extinction now or that is likely to become extinct during the 21st century if current population trends continue.

Epilimnion The surface layer of a lake through which sunlight penetrates and where lake plankton and plankton-feeding fish will be found.

Eutrophic A word to describe nutrient rich water that produces large amounts of plant and animal fish foods, but that might suffer low oxygen levels in hot summer weather. It is normally used in reference to lakes.

Eutrophication The enrichment of water though the addition of nutrients, usually from agriculture, or from industrial and sewage outfalls. Very clean water species, such as trout and grayling, might be replaced by species such as bream or roach and in extreme cases all fish are killed. It can be used in reference to any body of water.

Feral Fish that are not native, but have been introduced and formed breeding populations, such as rainbow trout throughout Europe and bream in Ireland. See also INDIGENOUS.

Fry Young fish, which are not long hatched. At this stage, they are feeding, but have not yet attained the adult life style.

Gammarid, *Gammarus* Small (to 15mm long) freshwater (also brackish and marine) shrimps that are conspicuously flattened along the sides. They constitute a major source of fish food in rivers and estuaries.

Gill, Gill cover, Gill raker The gill cover (or operculum) covers the gills, which are the fish respiratory organs. Each gill consists of a bony, V-shaped bar with long, red filaments (rays) on one side that extract oxygen from the water and spiky rakers on the other side. The structure and number of rakers are important in identifying some species, such as shads. See page 20 for fish structure.

Hybrid The progeny from the eggs of one species that have been fertilised by sperm of another species.

Ice Age relict An isolated population of a species in a site, usually a lake, which was home to that species during or immediately after the last Ice Age, and away from areas where most members of that species now live. For example, most pollan now live in Arctic Siberia and Canada, but they also occur in Irish loughs.

Indigenous A fish that is native to a particular country or region. For example, the largemouth bass is indigenous to North America and has been introduced into Europe, and the carp is indigenous to eastern Europe and has been introduced into western Europe. See also FERAL.

Keel, Keeled In some fishes, such as the rudd, the sides meet to form a very sharp ridge running along the belly. This ridge is known as a keel and the belly is said to be 'keeled'.

Landlocked This refers to populations of a species that is usually ANADROMOUS, but which spend all its life in freshwater due to its location, such as populations of twaite shad living in lakes.

Larva The fish is a larva immediately after it has hatched, but before it has become free-living and feeds on other organisms. (A larva is known as an ALEVIN in SALMONIDS.) In the insect world, the larva is, for many species, the growing stage between egg and PUPA, a popular dietary choice for many fish.

Lateral line A sensory line running along the sides of the body. It is missing or broken in some species. See page 20 for fish structure.

Leptocephalus The FRY stage of eels.

Mayfly A common insect group and major fish food in clean rivers and lakes.

Mesotrophic This refers to waters that are moderately productive, usually lakes. See also EUTROPHIC.

Midge The commonest aquatic insect group, which is found in huge numbers in rivers, lakes and brackish lagoons and marshes.

Milt The liquid containing sperm that is shed by male fish.

Nape The junction between top of head and back.

Nocturnal Fish that are most active by night.

Nymph The immature stage of several aquatic insects, such as mayflies, stoneflies and dragonflies. Nymphs are a major source of food.

Oligotrophic Referring to unproductive waters, usually associated with mountain lakes or lakes in northern Europe, that are not surrounded by intensively farmed land or cities. See also EUTROPHIC.

Ostracod Almost microscopic crustaceans that are found on the bottom of rivers and lakes and in PLANKTON. Ostracods are a major source of food for recently hatched fry of many species.

Parr The main freshwater feeding stage of ANADROMOUS SALMONIDS; in non-migratory SALMONIDS, parr refers to immature fish that have not attained adult coloration. The word comes from the so-called oval 'parr marks' on the sides of the body.

Pectoral fins The pair of fins just behind the head. See page 20 for fish structure.

Pelagic This describes creatures living in the open water of sea or lakes, such as PLANKTONIC organisms and the fish that eat these organisms.

Pelvic fins The paired fins on the underside of fish. Also known as ventral fins. See page 20 for fish structure.

Plankton Microscopic or almost microscopic plants and animals that live in open water and drift with the current (although vertical movements are possible). It includes phytoplankton (plant plankton consisting mainly of algae called diatoms) and zooplankton (animal plankton consisting mainly of CLADOCERAN and COPEPOD crustaceans and the LARVAL stages of larger animals, such as crabs, aquatic worms and some fish).

Pupa A resting stage in insects that have a growing LARVAL stage. MIDGE and caddisfly pupae are eaten in huge numbers by fish as they swim to the surface to hatch into the adult stage.

Redd A nest made in gravel by female fish (usually SALMONIDS).

Riffle, Run Shallow, often boulder-strewn, lengths of river between deep pools. Run can also refer to the 'run-in' to a pool neck.

Salmonid A member of the salmon and trout family (*Salmonidae*).

Smolt The silver, young ANADROMOUS SALMONID that goes to sea.

Stonefly An insect group found only in the cleanest of lakes and rivers; an important fish food.

Sucker disc The mouthparts of lampreys.

Tail In fish, the tail refers to the body between vent (anus) and the base of the tail fin. See page 20 for fish structure.

Tubercles Tiny pimply growths on the skin, sometimes also on pectoral fins and back, found in the males, occasionally females, of many CYPRINID species. They are usually white or cream and often appear during the breeding season.

Vent
The anus of a fish normally situated before the ANAL FIN. See page 20 for fish structure.

Yolk sac
The food reserves held by the egg and utilised by the embryo fish. After hatching the LARVA often remains attached the egg site, feeding on the remains of its yolk. When it is exhausted it ceases to be a LARVA, becomes a FRY and swims in search of food.

Conversion chart

Lengths

1mm	1/25in
5mm	1/5in
1cm	2/5in
2cm	4/5in
3cm	1 1/5in
4cm	1 1/2in
5cm	2in
6cm	2 1/3in
7cm	2 3/4in
8cm	3 1/5in
9cm	3 1/2in
10cm	4in
15cm	6in
20cm	8in
30cm	12in (1ft)
40cm	1ft 4in
50cm	1ft 8in
60cm	2ft
70cm	2ft 4in
80cm	2ft 8in
90cm	3ft
1m	3ft 4in

Weights

1g	1/25oz
10g	2/5oz
50g	2oz
100g	4oz
1kg	2lb 4oz
10kg	22lb 8oz
100kg	225lb

Temperatures

25°C	77°F
20°C	68°F
15°C	59°F
10°C	50°F
5°C	41°F
0°C	32°F

Index

Page numbers in **bold** refer to those with illustrations

Acknowledgements

Stuart Carter would like to thank: Malcolm, most sincerely, for your enthusiastic support throughout this project; the Mitchell Beazley team, for your unquestionable patience; and Maj, a very special heartfelt thanks for your exceptional help and support . . . and for just being there for me . . .

Photographic acknowledgements

Endpapers Michel Roggo
2 Malcolm Greenhalgh
7 Oxford Scientific Films/Keith Ringland
8 Malcolm Greenhalgh
15 Malcolm Greenhalgh
16 Still Pictures/Adrian Aribib
17 Angling Times
18 Environmental Images
19 Malcolm Greenhalgh
25 Oxford Scientific Films/Breck P Kent
27 Dr Rainer Berg
33 Oxford Scientific Films
35 FLPA/W Meinderts/Foto Natura
39 NHPA/Agence Nature
43 Oxford Scientific Films/Colin Milkins
45 Michel Roggo
49 Michel Roggo
51 Michel Roggo
53 Michel Roggo
55 Oxford Scientific Films/
Andreas Hartl/Okapia
57 Michel Roggo
61 Dr Rainer Berg
63 Dr Rainer Berg
65 Dr Rainer Berg
67 Norwegian Forestry Museum/OT Ljostad
71 Michel Roggo
73 Nature Photo Agency/Varjo Markku
75 Bruce Coleman Ltd/Dr Eckart Pott
77 Dr Rainer Berg
79 Dr Rainer Berg
81 Michel Roggo
85 Dr Rainer Berg
91 Dr Rainer Berg

93 NHPA/Lutra
97 NHPA/Jeff Goodman
99 Oxford Scientific Films/Peter Gathercole
101 Dr Rainer Berg
105 NHPA/Dr Ivan Polunin
111 FLPA/W Meinderts/Foto Natura
115 Michel Roggo
119 Dr Rainer Berg
127 Oxford Scientific Films/Alastair Shay
133 Michel Roggo
135 Michel Roggo
139 Oxford Scientific Films/Attilio
Calegari/Overseas
143 Michel Roggo
145 Dr Rainer Berg
147 Dr Rainer Berg
149 Oxford Scientific Films/R L Manuel
153 Dr Rainer Berg
157 NHPA/EA Janes
159 Oxford Scientific Films/David Fox
161 Dr Rainer Berg
163 FLPA/DP Wilson
167 Michel Roggo
169 Dr Rainer Berg
173 FLPA/W Meinderts/Foto Natura
179 Bruce Coleman Ltd/Charles and
Sandra Hood
187 NHPA/Trevor McDonald